In a Glass Darkly

The Bible, Reflection and Everyday Life

Zoë Bennett
and
Christopher Rowland

scm press

Published in 2016 by SCM Press
Editorial office
3rd Floor, Invicta House,
108–114 Golden Lane,
London EC1Y 0TG, UK

SCM Press is an imprint of Hymns Ancient & Modern Ltd (a registered charity)
13A Hellesdon Park Road, Norwich,
Norfolk NR6 5DR, UK
www.scmpress.co.uk

British Library Cataloguing in Publication data

A catalogue record for this book is available
from the British Library

978 0 334 05422 1

Typeset by Rebecca Goldsmith
Printed and bound by
CPI Group (UK) Ltd

Contents

To the many students we have taught in Oxford, Cambridge, Newcastle upon Tyne, and elsewhere, who have been our fellow travellers in the venture of critical reflection on the Bible and on life.

Acknowledgements

The *dramatis personae* of this book, from the pages of the Bible to the most recent conversations with colleagues, are too long to list in a short preface. Both of us learned much from Nicholas Lash who taught us in Cambridge, and Tim Gorringe's friendship has been a constant encouragement, and we have greatly appreciated being enabled to see how Karl Barth deserves to be thought of as a contextual theologian. To colleagues in the Professional Doctorate in Practical Theology a great debt of gratitude is owed for friendship in the venture of exploring self-reflexivity and the centrality of practice in theological research – especially Elaine Graham, Stephen Pattison and Heather Walton. There are, however, some to whom we are particularly indebted for their advice and counsel in connection with the genesis of this book. Natalie Watson when she was at SCM Press commissioned the book and David Shervington took up the baton and shared his wisdom with us. We are grateful to Catherine Rowland for her meticulous work proofreading this text. Finally, to the many students we have taught in Oxford, Cambridge, Newcastle upon Tyne, and elsewhere, who have been fellow travellers in the venture of creative critical reflection on the Bible and on life, we dedicate this book.

Introduction

> Nowe we se in a glasse even in a darke speakynge:
> but then shall we se face to face
> (1 Corinthians 13.12, William Tyndale's translation, 1526)

> If the doors of perception were cleansed every thing would appear to man as it is: infinite.
> (William Blake, *The Marriage of Heaven and Hell*, 14, E39).

> [T]he greatest thing a human soul ever does in this world is to *see* something, and tell what it saw in a plain way. Hundreds of people can talk for one who can think, but thousands can think for one who can see. To see clearly is poetry, prophecy, and religion – all in one.
> (John Ruskin, in Cook and Wedderburn 1903–12, 5.333)

The deepest human knowing comes with being known. In this life human knowing is always partial, seen 'in a glass darkly' – as if in a riddle, an 'enigma' (Greek ἐν αἰνίγματι), or as William Tyndale translated the verse: 'Nowe we se in a glasse even in a darke speakynge.' We hope to see clearly, we hope to know truthfully, we hope to be known fully. We press on. Paul's contrast of the present and the future in 1 Corinthians 13. 12 gave us the title of our book. His contrast probably echoes that in Numbers

12.8 where the face-to-face encounter with God enjoyed by Moses contrasts with other prophets' more dimly perceived grasp of the truth: 'With him I speak face-to-face – clearly, not in riddles; and he beholds the form of the LORD.' The climax of John's vision of heaven on earth comes when the inhabitants of the New Jerusalem come face to face with God (Rev. 22.4). That face to face encounter contrasts with seeing 'in a glass darkly'. The double metaphor of mirror and riddle in Paul's words is missed by most modern translations: we see only in a glass or a mirror, but also we hear only in riddles. In fact Paul opens up the imagination with *three* metaphors for seeing, understanding and intimate communication – mirror, riddle and face. They are all tangled up together; they are all partial, unclear and riddling for us in this everyday life.

The Velázquez painting on the cover of the book captures so much of what we have written, showing how an image brings together so many themes and ideas with a focus words cannot match. First, there is the juxtaposition of the life of the servant girl in the kitchen in the foreground and in the background the biblical scene of the disciples eating with Jesus when he is made known in the breaking of bread (Luke 24.31). Second, the preparation of such meals as that in the supper at Emmaus has been the woman's lot day in and day out. Her seemingly backward glance at the leisurely conversation contrasts her life of drudgery, stooped as she is over her table, with the situation of those two men who enjoy their meal, and injects a note of critical reflection as we who view the image see a young woman labouring over her tasks. The foundation of our book has been the way in which such a juxtaposition of the Bible and life stimulates reflection on our world, not least the injustices in it, our complicity in that injustice and that which we take for granted, as the labour of others supports the ease of our lives. Finally, the scene is ambiguous: is the woman looking at a picture or through a window? It underlines that in this present age we see in a glass darkly and must always struggle with the 'darke speakynge' of both life and of the Bible. In this picture the artist sets up an interpretative space that enables us to reflect on the social dynamics of the contents of the scene and the way in which life and the Bible relate, thereby enabling the possibility of the 'darke speakynge' of both everyday life and the words of the Bible to illuminate each other.

In our childhood at funfairs we could have a laugh at ourselves as we viewed the distortions of our facial features and forms in some mirrors. We neither dwell in the New Jerusalem nor share the privilege of Moses, but like Paul see in a glass darkly. How we see as clearly as we can is what this book is about, and the variegated attempts that anyone who shares Paul's messianic conviction of glimpsing and embodying the new age here and now needs to explore. As one of the writers we engage with puts it: '[T]he greatest thing a human soul ever does in this world is to *see* something, and tell what it saw in a plain way.'

This book is about the quest to know and to live well: to know our fellow human beings, to understand the world we live in, to act within a hopeful horizon and to work for the good of human society. This quest is impossible without ongoing critical reflection on our own lives, on our own understanding and on the histories that have made us what we are and given us the commitments we have. We are bound to see and understand partially;

it matters to know what the 'parts' are that we are seeing, and how our *way* of seeing both reveals and distorts. This is an impossible goal in this 'everyday life', but it is nevertheless the goal that is set before us.

'For a human being the unexamined (unreflective) life is not worth living', as Socrates reputedly said (Plato, *Apologia* 38A). Much is written about 'reflective practice' these days; this book is about 'reflective life'. With what tools may we reflect on life? The ones that are to hand. What we seek to argue for and illustrate is that the Bible may be such a tool for Christians, and indeed for others too. For both of us the Bible has been a central element in the shaping of our lives. And therefore to reflect critically on the Bible in the light of life, and perhaps even more importantly to reflect critically on life in the light of the Bible, is integral to living a reflective life.

The subject matter of this book can be represented in a Venn diagram, itself an appropriate way of explaining theology given the way it helped a writer such as Joachim of Fiore (1135–1202) to understand the relationship between God and history.

The Bible and the Christian tradition, and our experience both personal and professional, are the two elements that we bring into mutual critical dialogue. We use each to ask searching questions of the other. Our methodology here is that of liberation theology and of critical correlation in practical theology, ways of doing theology that have much in common and which have deeply influenced both of us.

Joint authorship adds a third element of critical reflection. It is more about *how* we have written the book than *what* we have written in it, but it is an essential part of the conceptual framework of our book. The critical perspectives that our joint authorship has brought to the stories we tell of personal and professional experience are an integral part of the journey of 'reflective life'.

Furthermore, working together ('collaborative hermeneutic') has meant that we have had to wrestle with *differences* in how we interpret and live with the Bible which surprised us, as well as the *commonalities* which we expected. The act of comparison has unearthed hidden features of similarity and of dissimilarity: comparison offers fresh perspectives and fruitful contradictions, and so aids critical reflection.

The overlap between the three circles in the diagram opposite indicates how these basic elements have contributed to us finding a critical space, learning to be self-reflexive and allowing our different experiences to shed light on the Bible and the Christian tradition and what we have learned from it.

Introducing ourselves

Personal and professional experience will feature as a central element in the conceptual framework of this book; so we begin by introducing our contexts and ourselves. Christopher has recently retired as Dean Ireland's Professor of the Exegesis of Holy Scripture in the University of Oxford. Zoë is the Director of a Professional Doctorate in Practical Theology, with the Cambridge Theological Federation and Anglia Ruskin University. We have both found a space, however on occasions problematic and constraining, to do the work we are passionate about within the institutional framework of Higher Education and the Church in the UK.

Chapter 1 begins with our first intellectual and imaginative encounter, where Zoë wrote an essay as a graduate student on her supervisor Christopher's favourite topic – the Book of Revelation as a critique of ideology. As we have more recently co-written essays that span our disciplines of New Testament Studies and Practical Theology (Bennett and Rowland 2005; Rowland and Bennett 2006), we have continually learned from each other. Zoë brought to the table from feminist theology the insight, beyond Christopher's liberationist perspective, that at times the Bible itself might be the problem. Christopher enabled Zoë to grasp that the Bible was not just the object of critical reflection but a powerful tool of critique itself – enabling reflective life. Blake and Ruskin (Chapter 5) have respectively and jointly fired our imaginations, and exposed contraries in the act of comparison. In Chapter 8 we reflect in a focused way on the nature of our collaborative engagement in the writing of this book, but inevitably that cannot be separated from our previous history of intellectual collaboration.

But our involvement with the Bible predates for both of us our professional lives. Our backgrounds with the Bible were different, and yet in crucial ways they overlap. Christopher went to a low-church Anglican church in a working class area of Doncaster, sang in the choir and church, and organ music became a dominant feature of his teenage years. The influence of evangelicalism triggered a self-involving engagement with the Bible which has never changed, notwithstanding the love–hate relationship with its contents. Reading the Bible academically has never been sufficient. Indeed, he has always been convinced that it probably means that we misunderstand the nature of what we are reading if we end up using it as a source book for ancient history. Zoë doesn't recall ever opening a Bible until she went to an evangelical church youth group when nearly sixteen. For years the Bible meant words written on billboards outside churches, school scripture and Christmas carols. Christianity was viewed through the lenses of Tolkien's *Lord of the Rings* and C. S. Lewis's *Narnia* books, as an awe-inspiring and mesmerizing grand myth (*mysterium tremens et fascinans*, Otto 1950). Time in that youth group, and later in the university Christian Union, dimmed the mysterious and compelling vision, but grounded her in a working knowledge of the Bible for which she continues to be genuinely grateful. Only later, ironically after a period of disenchantment focused in a radical feminist critique, would the Bible itself become a mediator of imaginative vision.

The nature of this book

Our book is not about criticism but about the role the Bible plays in learning to be critical. To that extent it shares a common feature with a more conservative position in allowing 'the strange new world within the Bible' (to borrow the words of Karl Barth 1935, pp. 28–50) to be integral to the critical task. The difference is that, while we think that the Bible offers an important component in critical awareness for the reasons we set out, it is not the only tool *and itself requires criticism* (which puts us at odds with a more conservative ethos). As such this book is, as far as we are aware, a unique contribution to practical theology, not least because of the dual perspective and background offered by a book that is jointly authored by a biblical scholar and a practical theologian.

T. S. Eliot wrote of the need to 'remind ourselves that criticism is as inevitable as breathing, and that we should be none the worse for articulating what passes in our minds when we read a book and feel an emotion about it for criticizing our own minds in the work of criticism' (Eliot 1951, p. 3). Substitute 'practice of Bible reading' for 'reading a book' and we have an apt description of what we are trying to do in our book.

A key theme of this book is that the Bible has a part to play in thinking about life. Learning to be critical must take place in the midst of everyday life. The Bible can be a part of this process, in which it is not an authority to which we defer but a catalyst for change and a tool of reflection. As such, criticism is not something done *after* the day's work is done (though it may include that), but in the midst of life, as patterns of analysis and reflection become part of the habit of everyday living. We think that engaging with the Bible is a neglected way of developing a critical perspective. For this reason we have attempted to indicate the ways in which the Bible has been a resource to us, and how we have developed a critical awareness through it. To quote the words of the Brazil-based liberation theologian, Carlos Mesters, Christopher 'understands life by means of the Bible', while Zoë 'understands the Bible by means of life'.

Our backgrounds are in practical theology and biblical studies, but we have both explored how we can learn from the ways in which the Bible has been used in the past, and by others who have explored the way in which critical theology emerges from life rather than from the study. We bring to this subject a shared interest in what is commonly referred to as contextual theology (though as will become clear in the book we think all theology is necessarily contextual). We have both learned much from the psychotherapeutic tradition and the skills that it encourages – to be aware, to listen, and to analyse and discern the next steps.

We hope to stimulate readers' imagination to engage with the Bible, by showing how and why it has been important for us. That has meant learning what we call 'critical reflexivity', which above all else requires an acknowledgement that there is no Olympian place from which to do our criticism. We will look at an 'archaeology' of our own Bible reading history. Understanding *how* we already interpret and 'inhabit' the Bible in using it, and how it is already *in* us, is a good starting point. The archaeology of one's reading history is a means to an end. This is not introspection for its own sake. Rather it is an essential part of the task of teasing out our prejudices. Self-reflexivity is a crucial tool whereby we might live better lives. Criticism is not an optional extra in life but is central to our humanity: 'as inevitable as breathing'.

Socrates' words quoted earlier, 'for the human being the unexamined life is not worth living' (Plato, *Apologia* 38a), embody a conviction that we would want to endorse as we too go on our journey of finding ever-new ways of being self-reflexive. Being self-reflexive is an indispensable part of allowing 'the Poetic Genius … the Spirit of Prophecy' (Blake, *All Religions are One*) full rein to do its work of protest and imagination rather than getting caught up in a self-centred ego-trip. We want to find ways of becoming more critically self-aware in our lives, and the Bible may assist us in that. For us a 'wrong' interpretation of the Bible is one that promotes inhumane behaviour largely as a result of not being sufficiently critically reflective.

Writing about the task of discerning a critical space includes describing and reflecting on what it is like to live with (or even in) the Bible. We indicate why we have lived with the Bible for so long, why it has given us an intellectual framework that informs who and how we are and helps to carve out a critical space for us. So, in a sense, we want to explore that which is endemic in critical study in the humanities, and in the process try to broaden the notion of what constitutes criticism by suggesting that the Bible is not just the object of criticism but a means of practising it.

An important part of our somewhat different critical journeys has been learning from the way others have engaged with the Bible. Ruskin and Blake have meant much to us, and we would like to see them informing biblical interpretation more than they do. What we have learned from our discovery of the differing ways of engaging with the Bible is that developing a critical perspective will not just be a resort to familiar theoretical, doctrinal, or historical examples.

Whatever we have to offer arises out of how we have attempted over the years to reflect on the various ways in which the Bible has informed our lives and the ways in which we have sought to establish patterns of discernment to be able to reflect on this. We attempt to condense from these some guidance on developing good practice. Our major aim is the creation, articulation and cultivation of a critical space in which the theological tradition of which we are part informs what is going on, albeit in ways that are in an appropriate dialectical relationship with our context. This will enable the interpreting subject to see more clearly, and as a result make informed judgements. In this task we have come to expect theology, and biblical studies, to have their part to play, along with experience, in cultivating a critical perspective. There is no assumption that theoretical reflection, historical enquiry and sociological theory have no part to play in learning to be critical and reflective, but we have resisted giving them the dominant role in working out how it is we learn to be 'critical', in order to make space for illustrating how the Bible has been as much assistance as the human sciences. Our view is that the Bible itself can offer a contribution to criticism, but the negotiation of a critical perspective comes not by detachment, but by finding that everyday life can be informed by the Bible and equally illuminate what the Bible is about. The ancient saying *Solvitur ambulando* (it is solved as one walks) evokes well the way insight is gained through practice, and criticism emerges as much, if not more, in the doing as in the withdrawal from the doing. Finding critical space and perspective *in the midst of* the confusion of life is a perspective that sheds light on the particular character and context of life as it is lived, to enable that life and context to be better understood and managed. That is the focus of our thesis.

What we set out to do has much in common with the ways in which the discipline of practical theology works. The traditional 'pastoral cycle' is in itself potentially a model for critical discernment, and is often used as such. It is what Don Browning has referred to as working from practice to theory to practice (Browning 1991). For some, the Bible is the senior partner at the conversation table and takes precedence over other sources of knowledge. In this view the Christian tradition, mediated through a reading of the Bible that honours it as the privileged word of God to humanity, takes 'logical priority' (Swinton and Mowat 2006, p. 89). For others the Bible is too much of a 'hot potato'. They are reluctant to draw on biblical resources in their understanding and presentation of situations in real life, partly because the Bible has so often been used in an uncritical and oppositional way to cut short all discussion by proof-texting and 'Bible-bashing', and partly through a sense of clumsiness and 'deskilling' when they try to engage with the Bible critically (Cameron, Reader and Slater 2012, pp. 74–93). In fact, 'critical conversation' is at the heart of practical theology (Pattison 2000, pp. 135–48) and the interpreting subject is indispensable (Graham, Walton and Ward 2005; Leach 2007). Here we explore that self-reflexivity, that activity of the 'interpreting subject', more deeply, and specifically explore it in relation to the Bible.

We challenge the exclusive focus on the hegemonic detached readings that historically have been an episode in the history of biblical hermeneutics and which characterize much current scholarship. While we adopt some of the critical perspectives of such scholarship, our book retrieves an older kind of 'self-involving' engagement with the Bible. We do think that there is an ethical component to all of this and so wish to challenge the notion of the priority of Bible, tradition or church, which should be applied to situations. We want to commend the reverse process in which situations, including especially those that involve human relating, take priority, and institutions and traditions serve human flourishing. It is what 'the Sabbath was made for humans not humans for the Sabbath' (Mark 2.27) is all about. So it is a challenge to an 'applied theology' notion of practical theology, or indeed of *any* theology.

Our approach offers a means of thinking and critical reflection in which the Bible is less an object of criticism and more one component among several in a process of critical reflexivity. It is not that we have found some kind of privileged perspective, whether academic or otherwise, from which we can look down on life and texts, for there is no escape from the critical process taking place in the middle of things. Discernment is going to take place in the process of learning more about ourselves, our world and the ways in which we interpret the Bible. Each of us is formed in a particular time and place. For both of us the Christian story, warts and all, has continued to be a powerful stimulus as well as an irritant, though for differing reasons. It is part of the mix of what informs our critical perspective. The Bible has helped form us and continues to act for us in ambiguous ways.

We have both been formed by modern theology, but have become resistant to its bracketing out of the understanding of the personal and existential from the intellectual task. Equally, we have found ourselves deeply resistant to the siren voices of neo-orthodoxy, in whatever guise. It may seem strange in the light of such caveats to assert that we still want the Bible to be part of the critical mix. Distancing ourselves from the Bible would be like losing something that has been an indispensable tool for our lives. It is not the only tool we use but for us both it *must* be one of them for it is part of who we are. Bolstered as we have been by our historical study, we are confident that what we are attempting to do is not only worth doing but of use to a wider group of Christian practitioners. What we do is personal and 'self-involving', but all the time it seeks to be critical. It offers a possible model of how one may go about critical reflection. What we are seeking is akin to Ernst Bloch's 'educated hope', in which we can learn to discern and intervene in the midst of 'the darkness of the lived moment' (1986, i.290), informed by past experiences as well as by the growing ability to catch a glimpse of the world as a better place.

The argument of the book

The book offers worked examples that start from the particular, and arise out of the various ways in which the Bible has impacted on our lives, including our professional lives. We are going to show by way of examples that we have a complex personal history of interpretation, much of which even with our best endeavours we are not going to be able to grasp, and we offer an emerging critical and reflective exploration that has assisted our self-understanding. We give central attention to the text of the Bible itself, which involves a critically aware autobiography in understanding how we read the Bible. Linked with this is engagement with context – how this is integral to the Bible itself as well as to our ways of reading it; how text and life, tradition and experience, are inextricably intertwined. Interpretation and experience are embedded in our dealings with the Bible like the writing in a stick of rock.

Chapter 1 starts with the Book of Revelation for two reasons. First, we want to start by plunging into some actual biblical text, and to wrestle with how we have interpreted it and what it means to us, before we get into second order reflection on understanding the act of interpretation. Second, historically this is the first text we worked on together.

Chapter 2 charts the centrality of hope in the New Testament, and the role of eschatology in this. It addresses Paul's role as the first Christian contextual theologian seeking to explore the meaning of the life of the new age in the midst of the old.

In Chapter 3, Turning Points, we give concrete examples of fresh understandings of the Bible mediated through life experiences. Our starting points are in our own 'conversion' experiences, but the issues raised are of global importance – how can we speak of God in the contexts of oppression (Bonhoeffer, 1981, Letters to E. Bethge, 8 June 1944, pp. 324–9; Gutiérrez 1983, p. 57).

Chapter 4 is autobiographical in a different way. We write of deeply personal experiences (which are professional too), and examine the ways in which we in practice work with and interpret the Bible in our everyday lives. We interrogate our operant models of relating the Bible to life.

Our historical 'conversation partners' feature in Chapter 5. We explore how our work on two historical readers of the Bible,

William Blake and John Ruskin, have offered us a 'place to stand on', to enable us to view our own contexts. From these we have gained both critical distance and inspirational engagement. By way of reflection we will include comparison and contrasts between Blake and Ruskin, enacting the theme of critical comparison by each writing a letter to the 'conversation partner' of the other – Zoë to William Blake and Christopher to John Ruskin.

Moving into a different mode of writing, in Chapter 6 we consider more explicitly hermeneutical questions, and discuss how we learn to be self-reflexive. Examining the importance of ideological criticism in the Bible, and its modern form in the Marxist tradition, we consider the ways in which ideology indicates how ideas are intimately related to the struggle for power and hegemony, and particularly the ways in which ruling elites promote their values by recourse to 'ideologies' that are deemed to be natural or normal but in fact serve their interests. An element of this is the importance of self-knowledge alongside awareness of one's social context. And so we discuss analogies with psychotherapy, and also look at the Ignatian exercises.

Finally in Chapters 7 and 8 we draw together the threads that emerge from our extended exploration of our journeys with the Bible. Chapter 7 lays out the patterns of similarity; Chapter 8 lays out the tensions and differences.

This book is not about a 'model' of how to read the Bible, or how to live a reflective life. Rather we hope it will stimulate the imagination of its readers to reflect on their own life's engagement with the Bible, and on their own 'conversation partners'.

1
The Start of the Journey

Christopher

Apocalypse

One of the terrible icons of our generation was the sight of the burning twin towers and their destruction in New York on 11 September 2001. A tabloid headline the following day was just one word to accompany the view cross the Hudson River towards Manhattan: *Apocalypse*. That word conjured up many things, but one thing above all else – the end of the world. Apocalypse is the word that opens the Book of Revelation, itself full of images of destruction and disaster, but it is more than that – it is a revelation of things in heaven and on earth. Apocalypse is unveiling, unmasking, revealing that which is hidden (Rowland 2016a).

My intellectual journey began with an exploration of the central place that visions played in some parts of ancient Judaism and early Christianity. That experiential visionary background seemed to make sense of the visionary character of the Book of Revelation. John of Patmos believed that he had seen what Ezekiel had seen by the River Chebar (Ezek. 1; cf. Rev. 4–5), and saw visions of judgement and hope that spoke to his generation as much as Ezekiel's had spoken to

Jews in Jerusalem and Babylon centuries before. That view has stayed with me ever since I discovered the work of Gershom Scholem and his pioneering scholarship on the history of Jewish mysticism. The mystical dimension of 'apocalyptic', as well as the concern with the last days, is essential for understanding Christian origins. A work like the Apocalypse sets out to be prophecy, but it includes not only eschatology but also visions and revelations of another world, which has as much in common with the mystical tradition in Judaism as with Christianity (Scholem 1955; Rowland 1982). That has been a *Leitmotiv* of much that I have done ever since. My first book challenged the notion that apocalypse/apocalypticism was about the end of the world; and the implication of the book is that the way in which the term 'apocalyptic' is used can be understood by reference to the confusion between a definition of apocalyptic that concentrated on the form of the Book of Revelation (revelatory) and one that concentrated on the content of Revelation (the cataclysmic events, the angelic beings, the symbolism, numerology and predetermined series of disasters that had to precede the new age). As a result I questioned whether apocalyptic texts were primarily about eschatology or should rather be considered a peculiar form of theological epistemology alongside other ways of discerning the divine will.

At first it was the visionary character of apocalyptic that grabbed my attention, but the other side, found in the Book of Revelation, came more to the fore as I came to a greater appreciation of the fact that the hope for a different world order is central to early Christian belief and practice. I could not understand the New Testament without reference either to that hope for the future or the visionary mode that enabled the convictions of some of the key figures like Jesus and Paul to believe that God's purposes were in the process of fulfilment. I did not believe then, nor have I had reason to change my mind since, that early Christians believed that the world was going to end. They *did* believe, as did many contemporary Jews inspired by the prophets of the Hebrew Bible, that the world as they knew it, with the social and political arrangements that typified that world, was passing away and new and different arrangements would be accomplished. Both Jesus and Paul believed that they had a part to play in enabling that to happen. From that day forward apocalypse as vision and apocalypse as the unmasking of the powers of this age, the prophecy of their destruction and the hope for something different, have dominated my reading and writing. My perspective has since moved beyond the New Testament, and particularly Revelation, to other ages of Christian history, when men and women shared those visionary and eschatological convictions found in the Book of Revelation, the Apocalypse of Jesus Christ, were often inspired by reading and meditating upon that text.

The Book of Revelation is not only crucial to the understanding of the dynamics of Christianity but has also been extraordinarily influential down the centuries not least for the challenge it has posed for interpreters. It has been viewed with suspicion by some of the most important theological figures in Christian history – Luther being an obvious example – and has been frequently pushed to the margins of religious and intellectual life. As its opening word implies it is an apocalypse, a revelation or unveiling of divine secrets, not least about the consummation of all things, when the New Jerusalem is established on earth and God is all in all. But it is also a devastating 'unmasking' of the powers of the world. Its political critique, especially in Revelation 13 and 17–18, is inspired in particular by the Book of Daniel. So both Daniel and Revelation inspired later generations in their critique of the political arrangements of their own day.

The key to John's vision is when the Lamb that was slain shares the throne of God and becomes in turn the key to the meaning of history (Rev. 4–5). The values of the world are turned upside down as the meaning of the messianic promise is here interpreted by the vision of the Lamb that was slain. The story of the Lamb bearing the marks of slaughter, Jesus, who suffered a violent death at the behest of a Roman governor, has become the lens through which history is viewed, as political power and the culture of Babylon in the world is also unmasked (Rev. 13 and 17).

William Blake saw the way the story of Jesus in the pages of the New Testament offered a pattern that put questions about the emerging conformity and its preoccupation with difference and separation. This story has gone on challenging and inspiring people down the centuries. Indeed, he read the Book of Revelation not as a map of the end of the world, like many modern Christians (and indeed many did in Blake's own day), but as a way of understanding an unjust world better and re-imagining the ways in which its wrongs may be righted. Heaven on earth and turning the world as we know it upside down is what Blake beckons us to.

Apocalypse involves both epistemological and, in the case of the Book of Revelation, eschatological elements. Apocalypse is about vision; it is about offering a different perspective on things, throwing into sharp relief the shortcomings of present arrangements and beckoning those who can catch a glimpse of this to work for something different. Vision and the horizon of hope complement each other, offering a means of critique, a glimpse of what could be different and an exhortation to begin to live differently. The visions of Jesus, of Paul and of John of Patmos lead to a different perspective on the present, prompting prophetic protest, tentative experiments anticipating a different way of being, so not solely a critical perspective but also the exploratory implementation of a different kind of social arrangement, which is not just for an elect group, because it is believed to be hope for humanity. John's visions are not prescriptive. Because they are expressed in figurative language, like metaphors, they may jolt us out of our complacency. They evince, to borrow Blake's words, 'the Poetic or Prophetic character', which prevent the 'repeat [of] the same dull round over again' (*There is No Natural Religion*, Version B, Conclusion, E3).

Apocalypse as vision of death and destruction, and as the unmasking of the powers of this age, is at work in the catastrophe that was 9/11. Whether that revelation of the state of things can yield something different depends on our willingness to see, judge and act appropriately. That involves repentance, learning from the mistakes of our prejudice, self-centredness and hubris and being willing to work for a world that reflects the Kingdom of God where people will hunger no more, and thirst no more and like God we will wipe away every tear from the eyes of those who weep (cf. Rev. 7.16–17).

Zoë and I are not very different from most people in thinking that the Book of Revelation is not an easy read in terms of its symbolism and its content. Nor in its demand: the way of the prophet is hard. There is little comfort in bearing witness, as Revelation 11 makes clear. Yet this is a text that we have found has stimulated our imaginations in different ways as our pieces reflect. Its importance in the context of what we are seeking to explore will be apparent as the book progresses. Like many others down the centuries we have found in its stark critique of the politics of its day and its culture a disturbing and uncomfortable aspect of the Christian message which can get buried under more sentimental words and phrases and more constricted understanding of what passes for gospel. But there is something about its visionary critique of the values of this age, which is a perennial reminder of the challenge that faces us all, not least those who identify with the Lamb who was slain. Marx helped me understand apocalyptic visions as a critique of ideology. The appeal of Revelation's visions to our creative imagination contains a criticism that is searching and powerful. The stark contrasts that are set up throughout the book between heaven and earth, and between Babylon and Jerusalem, themselves beckon the reader to alternative perspectives on the status quo.

We admit that we could have got to where we have in exploring the nature of self-reflexivity in all its aspects without reading the Book of Revelation, but it was part of a Bible that was in our bloodstream and so was integral to our own formation and thinking. *Mutatis mutandis*, in its own way and in its own time and place, its evocative and compelling images, seen in the glass of vision, offer another story of how things might be. It is just that – a story, an evocation – not a prescription. It summons its readers to share that different perspective and to bear witness to the inadequacies of the present in the light of the possibilities to come. Unlike in the Pauline literature, there is little understanding of a gathered community with its embryonic rules and sense of community, only a group of prophets whose vocation is to bear witness to the reality of the impoverished state of the present and how it might be different when heaven comes on earth and sorrow and sighing flee away.

Zoë

'A magnificent call to the imagination'

> [I]n writing an essay which required a close reading of the Book of Revelation, I took off from the secondary material and found myself journeying in the primary stuff of the text, analysing its imagery: images of intimacy, of power, blood, threat and fear, images of nakedness and riches, the human and divine violence subverted and deconstructed by the central image of the slain lamb. My imagination was seized by this text, not as a detailed *de*scription of future events, nor as a propositional

> *pre*scription for living, but as a tremendous and ambiguous invitation to see and to act differently – a magnificent call to the imagination. (Bennett 2016, pp. 25–6; see also Bennett and Gowler 2012, pp. 1–16; Rowland and Bennett 2006)

In the story of my relationship with the Bible, how it has informed me as a theologian and how I engage with it in my life and work, the Book of Revelation features prominently. A particular historical context was the initial occasion of this transformative encounter with the Book of Revelation – the writing of an essay as a postgraduate student.

The question I was addressing in my paper was: 'As an ancient form of the critique of ideology and an essential part of the maintenance of a theological dimension to our world, how far does the apocalyptic tradition as manifested in the Book of Revelation support this view?'

I perceived that the critique of ideology was exercised with great subtlety and vitality through the use of imagery. What was it that seized my imagination in those images? Why were they so transformative?

To be true to the experience I am describing I start this discussion by plunging straight in to the text itself. The Book of Revelation is full of images – images that get their power from evocations of the past, from sharp analogies with the present, and from performative visions that challenge and terrify, but most of all engender courage and hope.

Images of power – of throne and kingship and of destruction are used to evoke God's ultimate power and to set up an alternative locus of power in a fragmented universe. The keys of Death and Hades, the seven stars in Christ's right hand, trumpets, thunder and lightning – the book is reeling with images of power, strongly reinforcing God's claim to ultimate sovereignty, and also drawing the sting of final fear from the powers of this world. *Images of threat and fear* reinforce the power images. At the fall of Babylon: 'they will stand far off, in fear of her torment' (Rev. 18.10). Prayers rise like smoke, as smoke will rise later from the ruined city, and fire is thrown down in judgement:

> And the smoke of the incense, with the prayers of the saints, rose before God from the hand of the angel. Then the angel took the censer and filled it with fire from the altar and threw it on the earth; and there were peals of thunder, rumblings, flashes of lightning, and an earthquake. (8.4–5)

Such imagery is, however, inextricably linked with *images of sacrifice and suffering* – the Son of Man, the Lamb slain. When Christ says, 'as I myself conquered' (3.21) he is referring to his enduring of suffering to the end. This identification of the ultimate source of power as weak and suffering destabilizes and deconstructs a reading of the Book of Revelation which simply sets up a dualistic scenario in which evil powers are conquered or trumped by a stronger but equally ruthless destructive divine power.

The most striking image of threat is the 'wrath of the Lamb' (6.16). This derives much of its power from its apparent contradiction, almost toppling into nonsense. But not quite:

its bizarre quality reveals a hidden sense of menace while at the same time accepted categories are broken open.

> See, the Lion of the tribe of Judah, the Root of David, has conquered, so that he can open the scroll and its seven seals.
> Then I saw between the throne and the four living creatures and among the elders a Lamb standing as if it had been slaughtered … (Rev. 5.5–6)

As 'the wrath of the Lamb' the image may carry menace, but as an image of the Lamb by the throne 'standing as if it had been slaughtered' it witnesses to a very different form of power, a power that deconstructs the game of 'whose power of destruction is the stronger'.

Images of blood carry an interconnected set of references that hold both poles of the Lamb imagery – menace and suffering sacrifice, judgement and redemption – and draw into the picture a third element: the martyred faithful.

What happens here is fascinating, as a standard 'atonement' formula – 'who loves us and freed us from our sins by his blood' (1.5) – becomes combined with blood as a symbol of vengeance and destruction – 'So the angel swung his sickle over the earth and gathered the vintage of the earth, and threw it into the great winepress of the wrath of God. And the winepress was trodden outside the city, and blood flowed from the winepress, as high as a horse's bridle, for a distance of about two hundred miles' (14.19, 20). Then a third image is added: blood as a symbol of martyrdom. In 6.10 blood connects martyrdom and vengeance: 'Sovereign Lord, holy and true, how long will it be before you judge and avenge our blood on the inhabitants of the earth?' In 7.14 martyrdom is joined with the idea of Christ's death: 'they have washed their robes and made them white in the blood of the Lamb'. In 12.11 – 'but they have conquered him by the blood of the Lamb and by the word of their testimony, for they did not cling to life even in the face of death' – all three ideas, the blood of Christ's sacrifice, martyrdom, and the overcoming of evil, are interconnected. By 16.6 – 'because they shed the blood of saints and prophets, you have given them blood to drink. It is what they deserve!' – and even more so 17.6 – 'I saw the woman, drunk with the blood of the saints and the blood of the witnesses to Jesus' – the blood of martyrdom and the blood of vengeance are specifically combined in one metaphor; and by 19.13–15 the same has happened to the blood of Christ's sacrifice and the blood of judgement:

> He is clothed in a robe dipped in blood and his name is called The Word of God. And the armies of heaven, wearing fine linen, white and pure, were following him on white horses. From his mouth comes a sharp sword with which to strike down the nations, and he will rule them with a rod of iron; he will tread the winepress of the fury of the wrath of God the Almighty.

By means of this use of imagery two results are achieved. First, a pattern of mutual evocation is set up whereby any of the three elements – Christ's sacrifice, martyrdom, judgement

– carries overtones of the other. Second, the symbol of Christ's sacrifice, which on its own does not necessarily play this role, is brought into the service of the critique of ideology. It does this by demonstrating the cost of discipleship and the significance of witness as a continuation of the ultimate martyrdom in Jerusalem, and a judgement on the powers of evil. Thus the ideology of the 'evil empire' is exposed, and a vision of hope offered to those who suffer for their witness to the slain Lamb.

Two further sets of imagery carry the momentum of judgement and hope – *images of nakedness and riches* and *images of intimacy*.

Nakedness is contrasted with fine clothing and wealth:

> 'Alas, alas the great city,
> clothed in fine linen,
> in purple and scarlet,
> adorned with gold,
> with jewels, and with pearls!
> For in one hour all this wealth has
> been laid waste!' (18.16–17)

It is not only the bankruptcy and nakedness of the great city which are exposed, but also that of the churches. From the start of the book (letter to Laodicea, 3.17–18) nakedness and riches are interconnected, and also linked to the unmasking of reality:

> For you say, 'I am rich, I have prospered and I need nothing.' You do not realize that you are wretched,

> pitiable, poor, blind, and naked. Therefore I counsel you to buy from me gold refined by fire so that you may be rich; and white robes to clothe you and to keep the shame of your nakedness from being seen.

White or clean robes recur as a theme, linked with purity and with the 'righteous deeds of the saints', linked also with hope for a different order and for life in God: 'I saw under the altar the souls of those who had been slaughtered for the word of God ... They were each given a white robe and told to rest a little longer' (6.9–11); 'Blessed are those who wash their robes, so that they will have the right to the tree of life' (22.14).

Images of intimacy gather momentum as the Book of Revelation progresses. From first to last these images co-exist with images of threat, fear and judgement. In the first three chapters Christ stands in the midst of the churches; to encourage, but also to judge. His close presence is both intimacy and threat, as is also seen in 11.19 – the open temple and the ark of the covenant are embedded in a terrifying storm: 'Then God's temple in heaven was opened, and the ark of his covenant was seen within his temple; and there were flashes of lightning, rumblings, peals of thunder, an earthquake, and heavy hail.'

In 7.15–17 we have a foretaste of the end – of the temple, of shelter, the shepherd, the comforter and provider. By the final chapters of the book images of intimacy begin to run riot: bride, sons, servants, the river and the tree of life. The throne of God and of the Lamb is in the midst of the city (the double unity of Christ and God, Christ and humanity), now the dwelling of God is with human beings. There is no need of a temple – Israel's image of intimacy; or of the sun – creation's image of intimacy; the kings of the earth will find the gates of the city never shut – the Gentile's image of intimacy.

Reflections

We have started with the Book of Revelation for several reasons. It establishes the centrality of the biblical text itself for this book; it embeds our work autobiographically in our contexts; and it indicates the foundational role of both imagination and the critique of ideology in our life and work with the Bible.

We have both located the genesis of our interest in the Book of Revelation in an academic context. This is to be expected, as the 'academy' *is* our context. Some nuance is, however, needed here. The academy has been for Christopher both home and a strange place. His work on Jewish mysticism, on apocalyptic and on visionary experience, of which studies on the Book of Revelation have been an integral part, has offered him places to stand outside the mainstream of the academic guild of biblical studies.

For Zoë, this imaginative engagement as a way of entering into the text was not undertaken in a devotional context such as *lectio divina*, or the Ignatian exercises, but also in an academic context. The systematic and hermeneutical teasing out of the images was embedded in a scholarly essay. Did the academic context itself provide a safe space to explore scripture? A space in which she could set aside her need to make scripture say something safe and acceptable, because she could step aside from the 'house of authority' which required her to love the Bible, be formed by the Bible, and act by the Bible. The academic context in which we have both worked for much of our lives has offered in a contradictory way both constraint and freedom.

This academic context made it safe to look at a book of the Bible using the kinds of tools, and engaging the kind of in-depth imaginative process, which she would have used in her schooldays to read and explore literary pieces. This kind of diving in and opening up – self to the text and the text to self – had characterized her best times of academic engagement as a younger person, in the heyday of school (much more significant to her education in the main than university was).

This question does not only arise in relation to the Bible. Consider the following comment, in reflection on two unpublished essays written by the poet Ted Hughes, at school aged 17 – essays that contained no reference to secondary literature, but just searing imaginative, insightful and confident declarations of response to John Donne's poetry and to the idea of Excitement.

> The essays are written by someone who, by the age of 17, had worked out what he thought about both life and literature and had found his own critical voice. They make one reflect upon whether the teaching of English in schools and universities has actually been going backwards rather than forwards. What marks would such essays be given now? (Barrington, Bennett and Wymer 2014)

As Ted Hughes did with Donne, Zoë just started reading and responding to those images in the Book of Revelation.

Working on the Book of Revelation was the first piece of academic work we did together. This makes it an ideal place to start.

The Book of Revelation embodies the power of scripture to furnish us with 'another view'. In Revelation not only are the ways of God revealed to humanity but the ways of human beings on earth lie open to God. In fact there is a sort of double 'unmasking'; the unmasking of human reality undertaken from God's point of view, which then is revealed back to us. This indicates a model, not only of the seer looking into the opened heaven, but of God looking into the opened earth and the seer enabled to look on with him. Thus the heavenly visions function like a pair of spectacles through which we may see the realities of this world better, and have hope for a better world. That is to say they furnish us with a critical space.

2
The Horizon of Hope

> For the New Testament scholar apocalyptic is a basic phenomenon of the discipline. Without it the history of early Christianity cannot be understood … Apocalyptic, Christianly understood, is a theology of liberation and salvation, not of anxiety. (Käsemann, 2010, pp. 4–5)

'The Kingdom of God has drawn near'

These words from the distinguished German scholar Ernst Käsemann summarize a position that has to be a *sine qua non* for any understanding of the New Testament's writings. The most significant discovery in modern New Testament scholarship has been the realization that without grasping the centrality of hope for a new age, we shall not understand the New Testament (Rowland 2002). But it is important to recognize that for a century or so the early Christian hope, similar to contemporary Jewish hopes, was for a new era in the life and ordering of *this* world, when, to quote the words of Revelation 11.15: 'The kingdom of the world has become the kingdom of our Lord and of his Messiah.' Of course, the theme of promise and fulfilment has been endemic to Christian theology throughout its history and eschatological ideas and millennial movements have had their part to play in the formation of Christian thought, but that the message of Jesus is to be understood in the light of hopes for a new era in the life and ordering of this world is a distinct contribution of modern exegesis. It was the discovery of the Ethiopian Apocalypse of Enoch and the gradual process of seeking to comprehend the biblical sources in the light of such ancient material that gave a different perspective. So, for example, in the writing of Albert Schweitzer eschatology was not just one component of Christian theology but the very motor of the development of Christian thought. The dramatic opening words, attributed to Jesus in the Gospel of Mark, summarize it: 'the time is fulfilled; the Kingdom of God has drawn near' (Mark 1.15). It is the clarion call that echoes throughout the rest of the Synoptic Gospels.

While there have been attempts to circumvent the reality of eschatology in the New Testament, the eschatological mind-set pervades every page. In the Synoptic Gospels, whether it be the Son of Man coming on the clouds of heaven, Jesus' vow of abstinence from wine until he drinks it again in the Kingdom of God, or the link between the overcoming of the powers of evil as a sign that the 'Kingdom of God has overtaken you' (Luke 11.20), the gospels are pervaded with traditions whose meaning is only really comprehensible in the light of the vibrant Jewish hope of the coming of a new age of justice and peace. What is distinctive about the New Testament writings as compared with contemporary texts from their Jewish milieu is that this is not just a hope for the future but an expectation in some in the process of realization.

It is that perspective that pervades the Pauline letters also. So, in 1 Corinthians 1.18, Paul refers to those who reason with the logic of the cross as people who are '*being* saved'; similarly, in Romans 1.16–17, in the gospel 'the righteousness/justice of God is *being revealed* through faith for faith; as it is written, "The one who is righteous/just will live by faith."' Here we have evidence of one who believed himself to be in some sense an agent of eschatological fulfilment in his role as 'apostle to the gentiles' (Gal. 1.16), but believed that the signs of that new age were there to be seen by those who had faith and that the inexorable process of fulfilment had begun, however long its completion might take. For Paul, key alongside the belief that the eschatological prophetic spirit was again active was the fact that an item of eschatological hope, the resurrection of the dead, had already happened in the case of Jesus of Nazareth and was a foretaste of the fulfilment still to come.

Jesus, the bearer of hope

Jesus resembled prophetic figures mentioned briefly by the first-century Jewish historian Flavius Josephus in his writings (e.g. *Antiquities* xx. 97; 167–72; 185–8; *Jewish War* vi. 285). The activity of these prophets, as was the case with Jesus, prompted large crowds which saw in their persons and actions new signs of God's liberating activity. Jesus' assertion of the nearness of the Kingdom of God, however, put him in a different position from another Jesus mentioned by Josephus (*Jewish War* vi. 300–9), whose prophecies of doom led to his arrest (though ultimately he was released by the Romans as a harmless eccentric). Jesus of

Nazareth's message was of hope not of doom.

Jesus was closely connected with John the Baptist, who was executed for subversion by Herod Antipas (Josephus, *Antiquities* xviii.116–19). John appears to have seen himself as the herald of a decisive moment in God's purposes, and this seems to have provided the context for Jesus' own activity and his convictions about his peculiar place in the divine economy. Jesus and his immediate band of followers were itinerants, supported by local hospitality and possibly also a few wealthy sympathizers. Jesus attracted attention from the Galilean peasantry because of his wonder-working, which he saw as a sign of the imminence of the messianic age, the coming of the Kingdom of God on earth, and because of his proclamation of God's bias towards the poor and insignificant, and other teaching that drew more on traditional wisdom as the learned debates of the contemporary teachers.

Whether or not Jesus saw himself as the Davidic messiah, a blend of intense visionary experience and a sense of vocation persuaded Jesus to move from Galilee to Jerusalem, the metropolitan centre of the Jewish religion. A large popular following in the volatile atmosphere of Jerusalem at pilgrimage time was enough to set him at odds with the priests. The entry into the city (according to the Synoptic Gospels) and the 'cleansing' of the Temple, were probably seen as threats to public order which provoked a response from those in power (so Mark 11.18; John 11.47–53). As a result there was a conflict between Jesus and the semi-autonomous hierarchy in Jerusalem backed by Roman colonial power. Neither they nor the Romans needed to take direct action against Jesus, for, as the result of a defection from his group, Jesus was captured and executed without any armed struggle. He died as a subversive at the hands of the Roman colonial power.

'He fell foul of the high priestly authorities in a politically unstable Jerusalem because he did the wrong thing in the wrong place at the wrong time', so Geza Vermes said (1993, p. x). 'The wrong thing in the wrong place at the wrong time.' The fact that Jesus was in Jerusalem on that fateful Passover was, according to the gospels, not just because of his piety, but because of an impulse that set him on that journey to Jerusalem and thence to his death. The crisis brought about by his presence there was in part engineered by him. He was not simply a victim of circumstances, having unwittingly stumbled into a situation that proved to be fatal. In the New Testament gospels Jesus is presented as being an *agent* of the Kingdom of God, thereby being the fulfiller of the Jewish hopes for a new world. His final journey to Jerusalem was a politically provocative act.

The stories that the first Christians told about him were of one who fractured the power of the Temple (cf. Mark 15.38), the central economic motor, and ideological symbol, of Jewish society. He challenged the ideology of the Jewish hierarchy and their supporters who managed the Temple in the words of the Johannine Jesus, 'my kingdom is not from this world. If my kingdom were from this world, my followers would be fighting to keep me from being handed over' (John 18.33–36). Jesus advised his disciples: 'You know that those who are supposed to rule over the Gentiles lord it over them, and their great men exercise authority over them. But it shall not be so among you; but whoever would be great among you must be your servant' (Mark 10.42–44).

Paul, the strategist of hope

The title 'strategist of hope' is deliberate. What Paul has in common with Jesus is hope and its partial realization. As compared with the gospel stories, however, what we have in the Pauline letters is far more detail about what that means in practice. Jesus is represented as teaching his disciples, but the content of that teaching is allusive, in parables and related sayings and in predictions of his imminent death; but what led him to go up to Jerusalem and how the kingdom of God might come is left unclear. The disciples just accompany him. The disciples are companions following Jesus in the way (Mark 9.34; 10.32; Luke 9.51, 57). What they end up doing is put succinctly by Thomas in John 11.16: 'Let us also go, that we may die with him.' Also, narrative by its very nature is less prescriptive than the kinds of instructions and embryonic doctrinal system we find in Paul's letters. The latter, therefore, give us a glimpse of an activist, a strategist enabling individuals as they coalesce in community to learn to live as followers of the Messiah.

Paul the apocalyptic visionary: apostle of the Messiah on a cosmic stage

Paul's messianic convictions crystallized for him primarily as the result of an apocalypse of Jesus Christ. He identified the heavenly being he saw in his apocalypse with Jesus the Christ. Apocalypse is the first step followed by reflection on Scripture and tradition. Experience came first followed by reflection. Paul discerns the Jesus whom he saw in an apocalyptic vision as the fulfilment of prophetic hope, the one who ushered in the messianic kingdom by his life, death and resurrection. Paul's sense of himself is nowhere better communicated than in his account of the dramatic event that turned his world upside down in Galatians 1.11–16. His self-description owes much to earlier emissaries of God, Isaiah of the exile and Jeremiah. The words from Jeremiah that are quoted relate to Paul's place in the plan of God and his being marked for this task: 'But when God, who had set me apart before I was born and called me through his grace, was pleased to reveal his Son to me, so that I might proclaim him among the Gentiles' (Gal. 1.15–16 cf. Jer. 1.5 and Isa. 49.1).

Elsewhere, even allowing for rhetorical exaggeration, Paul sees his action, and that of his colleagues, as being on a very public, indeed cosmic, stage: 'God has exhibited us apostles as last of all, as though sentenced to death, because we have become a spectacle to the world, to angels and to mortals' (1 Cor. 4.9). In a passage written by one of his earliest and most ardent apologists, Paul tells King Agrippa that his activity 'was not done in a corner' (Acts 26.26). Such views are entirely consistent with his sense of calling, as one who in some sense continued the prophetic witness of Isaiah and Jeremiah and whose task it was to be an agent of the demonstration of the reign of God on earth, and so reveal that Jesus was the 'bearer of hope'. So, in 1 Corinthians 2.4–5, Paul writes, 'My speech and my proclamation were not with plausible words of wisdom, but with a demonstration of the Spirit and of power, so that your faith might rest not on human wisdom but on the power of God' (also Gal. 3.1, where Paul says that before the very eyes of the Galatians, Jesus Christ was publicly portrayed as crucified in Paul's own body, cf. Gal. 6.17).

The tension between culture and society, 'the world as it is' and the hope for the Kingdom of God on earth and its necessary anticipation in concrete practices pervades the Pauline letters. The present had become a time of fulfilment: 'Behold, now is the acceptable time; behold, now is the day of salvation' (2 Cor. 6.2).

Members of the messianic community are not merely believers in the messiah but are in some sense clothed with the messiah's person: they put on Christ like a garment (Gal. 3.27; Rom. 13.14). They have the Spirit of Christ, the messiah dwelling in them (Rom. 8.9; Gal. 4.6–7). The relationship between the individual and the collective is close: 'you are all one in Christ Jesus' (Gal. 3.28). Paul's use of language of *koinonia* indicates that those in that fellowship are to be understood as living in 'partnership'. God calls believers into 'partnership' with Jesus Christ (1 Cor. 1.9) rather than partnership with demons (1 Cor. 10.20). This partnership motif dominates his letter to the Philippians, which points out regularly how the Philippians are partners in the gospel (Phil. 1.5); partners with Paul in grace (1.7); partners of the Spirit (2.1); how God has granted them not only to believe in Christ but also suffer on his behalf (1.29). Paul is a partner in Christ's sufferings (3.10), and the Philippians are partners with Paul in his distress (4.14) and have been partners with Paul in giving and receiving (4.15).

Paul's most explicitly apologetic and autobiographical letter is Galatians. Whether it was his earliest letter or not, it is an extraordinary defence of the basis of his authority, his understanding of his relationship to the past and his conviction that previous ways of doing things had changed. We see at work here not an appeal to a tradition of teaching stretching back to Moses but an authority based on his experience of apocalypse, an 'unveiling' of Jesus Christ, just as was the case with John the seer (Rev. 1.1). That experience has consequences for the recipients of the letter and the retrospective assessment of his ancestral tradition. Paul makes it absolutely clear that he is an agent not because he has been commissioned by humans but because of an apocalypse of Jesus Christ. Paul rejects the idea that he is merely the intermediary of the church in Jerusalem and therefore subordinate to their dictates and so turns to the vexed issue of the condition for admission of Gentiles into the messianic community. Paul's visionary experience laid the foundation for the conviction that the position of the Law of Moses had changed in the divine economy now that the messianic age to come had dawned even if it meant seemingly abrogating the rules of admission, which had for centuries applied to those who espoused Judaism. That basic datum turned his world upside down, and was the basis for his extraordinary career bringing this message to non-Jews. The conviction is messianic, in the sense that promises are being fulfilled and a new age has come, with 'redemption from the present evil age' a real possibility (Gal. 1.4). Paul believed that the messianic age had come and that there was a new dispensation available for a number of Gentiles who could become children of Abraham by means of faith in the Messiah.

Paul, the scriptures and community

Paul's strategizing of hope was not primarily theoretical but was worked out and embodied in the living communities with which he was involved and which are so often the addressees of his letters. Two commitments are vital to his work in the building up of communities: his reading of the scriptures and his engagement with experience. We see in his wrestling with this dual commitment no clear and unambiguous theoretical order of precedence, but the tension between tradition and experience, authoritarianism and antinomianism embodied in Paul himself.

In the light of the advent of the Messiah the Jewish scriptures were read in the conviction that the age of the Spirit had come. Paul told the Christians in Corinth that passages in the Bible were in reality addressed directly to those fortunate to be alive when the decisive moment in history came about: 'Now these things happened to them as a warning, but they were written down for our instruction, upon whom the end of the ages has come' (1 Cor. 10.11). The present, therefore, has become the moment to which all the scriptures have been pointing and their meaning can only be fully understood with that insight that flows from acceptance of the Messiah. The internally driven knowledge of God is the appropriate motor by which to live in the divine life.

Paul was less a detailed exegete and commentator than a mystic, informed and inspired by the intersection of his own experience and the scriptures. The immediate apprehension of the divine through the Spirit is fundamental. One cannot read 1 Corinthians 2.10–16 without realizing that at most the interpretation of the Bible was ancillary to the convictions (in every sense of that word) provided by the divine Spirit, which also offered him the basis for the authority to speak and act as an apostle (agent) of the heavenly Christ, the steward of the divine mysteries (1 Cor. 4.1). Precedent and tradition seem to take second place to experience. Paul now read the Bible of his youth in the light of his messianic convictions.

The point at which Pauline Christianity and the bulk of

contemporary Judaism parted company was over whether or not it was possible to have an interpretation of Judaism without accepting the literal *implementation* of all the laws (e.g. circumcision) for matters of belief and, rather than use of it as a *general* guide for life, as Paul seems to suggest in Romans 15.4: 'For whatever was written in former days was written for our instruction' (cf. Segal 1990).

Despite his strong language in Galatians, Paul wanted to guarantee the central importance of the Law of Moses, principally as the witness to the messianic salvation that was now dawning. Even if Paul was opposed to the written law as the definitive embodiment of God's saving purposes (cf. 2 Cor. 3.6–16), the new life in Christ he commends means walking in newness of life (Rom. 6.4). If the letters are anything to go by, what is involved in this newness of life did not consist of many specific regulations, except to fulfil 'the law of Christ' (Gal. 6.2), or the obligation to love one's neighbour (Gal. 5.14; cf. Rom. 13.9), the latter being the fulfilling of the whole Law.

Nowhere does Paul's Jewish upbringing dominate as much as in the Corinthian correspondence. It is Paul the rabbi asserting himself at the expense of Paul the charismatic. Or put another way, it was all right for Paul to be a charismatic and a mystic but definitely not all right for anyone else to be given the kind of autonomy he claimed for himself, particularly if it differed from Paul's firmly held opinions. 1 Corinthians is similar to the emerging rabbinic restrictions on mystical experience which we find in the early rabbinic collection of legal opinions, the Mishnah (Mishnah Hagigah 2.1). But there are stringent qualifications on who should be allowed to participate in this kind of engagement, with dire warnings of the consequences for the uninitiated.

Paul asserted that the communion of the believer with Christ needed no intermediary, whether human or institutional, but also he seems to demand communal and political order based on obedience to a tradition or authorized individuals (Paul being chief among them). Rather than teaching obedience to a written code, Paul teaches his churches the practice of community discernment, where they 'prove through testing' what is the will of God (e.g. Rom. 12.1–2; 1 Thess. 5.21–22; Phil. 1.9–11; 2 Cor. 13.5; Eph. 5.10; discussed in Lewis 2005). Paul describes for them the pattern of Christ in Philippians 2.1–11 and then tells them in 2.12: 'work out your own salvation with fear and trembling …'. The community has to take responsibility for discerning the mind of Christ and discerning what faithfulness looks like in their particular contexts.

That said, Paul sometimes cannot help himself and he attempts to subvert the communal practice of discernment by determining what the outcome of the discernment process ought to be. 1 Corinthians is an especially good example of the tension that runs right the way through the Pauline corpus. Those who accept the Messiah can understand the true meaning of the scriptures and taste the goodness of God and the powers of the age to come. The scriptures have ceased to be the primary source of guidance for them. The indwelling spirit guides the believer, something that is set out in 1 Corinthians 2.10–16, where the role of the Spirit in the revelatory process is outlined (cf. Rom. 8).

A crucial move, however, is made in the last verse of 1 Corinthians 2, where we find the conviction, on Paul's part, that he and his companions are the ones who know the mind of Christ, in contrast to the Corinthian Christians. Paul speaks God's wisdom to the 'mature' (1 Cor. 2.6), which refers to those who, in his view, are walking in the ways of Christ, and pattern themselves on Paul (see, e.g. 1 Cor. 4.16–17; 11.1). The legacy of what Paul offered in terms of the scriptures and community is found in his words in 1 Corinthians 5–6, where the Corinthians are offered Mosaic-inspired injunctions without so much as a word of explanation, other than the authority of Paul (1 Cor. 5.3–5). Paul seemed intent on creating a holy Temple (1 Cor. 3.16; 6.19; 2 Cor. 6.14–7.1) – a purified space, mirroring the holiness of the Temple in the Corinthian community. Grave sins, including sexual sins, defiled the temple. If these sins are not expunged, God's presence will depart as will God. The injunction to be holy is a central concern of the purity codes (Lev. 10.10; 20.26). So, the sexual impurity had to be rooted out of their midst, just as it had to be out of the midst of the people of God, as it defiled the rest of the Temple of God which is now the Body of Christ. Here Paul put biblically inspired demand for holiness firmly on the nascent Christian ethical agenda.

Paul as community organizer: hope as contextual negotiation

Concern for his communities dominates the Pauline letters in the New Testament. There are many themes in these letters which are socially conservative, for example, Paul's words about the state (or, more accurately, 'the powers that be', Rom 13.1), and the role of women (e.g. 1 Cor. 14.33–4; cf. 1 Tim. 2.11–15). They exude pragmatism, the demonstration of the art of persuasion and occasional bouts of authoritarianism based on his visionary conviction. This helped lay the foundations of a pattern that was independent of what counted as mainstream Judaism with its pattern of life and worship and distinctive ideology.

This emphasis on the absolute determination to enable not disintegration but survival and community is put well by Slavoj Žižek. Strikingly, he compares Lenin and Paul, both of whom acted in such a way that their intervention changed the situation. He argues that Paul's conversion offered a model for the radical re-orientation of one's life. He became part of a minority community of solidarity and resistance to contemporary culture. In so doing he offered those who followed him a place that was on the brink of seeing something new:

> What matters to him is not Jesus as a historical figure, only the fact that he died on the Cross and rose from the dead – after confirming Jesus' death and resurrection, Paul goes on to his true Leninist business, that of organizing the new party called the Christian community. Paul as a Leninist: was not Paul, like Lenin, the great 'institutionalizer', and, as such, reviled by the partisans of 'original Marxism-Christianity'? Does not the Pauline temporality 'already, but not yet' also designate Lenin's situation between the two revolutions, between February and October 1917? Revolution is already behind us, the old regime is out, freedom is here *but* the hard work still lies ahead. (Žižek 2003, p. 9)

Paul sought to instill conformity to his injunctions and the *pattern* he offered, as the paradigmatic imitator of Christ (1 Cor. 11.1).

He sought to establish a degree of uniformity (1 Cor. 14.33). In this respect there is a thread that links the Paul of letters like Romans, Galatians and 1 Corinthians, especially the last mentioned, and the Paul of the Pastoral Epistles. So, Christianity gradually became an uneasy compromise between radicalism and conservatism.

The identity of Christianity finds many of its contradictory common features in the Pauline epistles. Linda Woodhead offers a typology of Christianity that includes a mystical type, a church type, and a biblical type, depending on how they embody and represent authority (2004). All these three aspects are present in what we find in the Pauline corpus, so that Christian identity in all its differing facets and emphases in different times, places and individuals, owes so much to the ways in which the Pauline texts have influenced later readers. The Pauline letters present us with a mix of the apocalyptic/visionary, the community organizer, and the authoritative biblical interpreter. A letter like 1 Corinthians is full of these different facets. Paul is at his most apocalyptic and his most authoritarian within a few pages. Thus, 1 Corinthians 2.6–16 outlines a mystical type, whereas by contrast in his instructions elsewhere, confronted as he appeared to have been with the consequences of the kind of mystical piety outlined in 1 Corinthians 2, Paul not only pulled rank and asserted his apostolic status but also drew on traditional Jewish ideas. As suggested, Paul's intention is to create a purified space. It is ethical advice that put the culture of holiness firmly on the emerging Christian ethical agenda. The ethos of passages like 1 Corinthians 3.16–17 and 6.18–19 have dominated Christian understanding ever since. Here is the moment when, to use Linda Woodhead's typology, the biblical trumps the mystical to promote the Church. But the mystical is as much a part of the Pauline legacy as numerous mystics, visionaries and antinomians down the centuries have perceived – and the promoters of Bible and Church have struggled to keep it in order or marginalize it.

The contextual nature of Paul's theology has been widely acknowledged in Pauline scholarship, underlining the occasional and time-bound situated-ness of what is written. But even in the most conservative passages, where Paul sought to keep women subordinate or talked positively about the divinely ordained 'powers that be', there is a recognition that, whatever change happened, that change had to take full account of the constraints of context. While today we may chafe at aspects of the advice that Paul gives, the ways in which Paul seeks to find a space not only for himself but also his churches to live different kinds of lives in the midst of a very different set of values is an amazing feat of survival and creative living. In effect what he achieved was to set up an alternative political commitment characterized by practical and administrative arrangements manifested in networks of communication and mutual support. Paul's collection for the poor in Jerusalem is one the earliest examples of this (Rom. 15. 25; 2 Cor. 8–9). It is a model for practical theology in any situation in its exploration and discernment of how best to exploit whatever spaces are available to offer a glimpse of what life in the Kingdom of God might be like. As 1 Corinthians, epitomized in chapter 13, makes clear, Paul above all was keen to ensure that mutual respect was encouraged (cf. Rom. 15.25–29; 2 Cor. 8–9). His activity, in person and in his letters, is a feat of ingenuity, improvization, survival and creative living to find a space, not only for himself, but also his communities, to explore different ways of living which anticipated the age to come. So, Paul is the epitome of the practical, contextual theologian. Even the Letter to the Romans, the nearest Paul gets to a systematic treatise, is shot through with the need to pave the way for a visit to people with whom he has had little contact. The recipients are treated to an extended apologia for his messianic convictions and how he bore witness to a vision of a different kind of public space. This letter lays out the requirement for those attracted by that messianic vision in order to explore how they actualized it here and now. It is all about how one lives in anticipation of a world where sorrow and sighing will flee away.

Paul was an apocalyptic rabbi, on the one hand a teacher who had a sense of authority and sought to impose what he thought on his communities, but on the other a man of vision, whose apocalyptic experience was the basis of his authority. Constrained by the limits of communication that confronted him as well as by his itinerant life-style, Paul inserted his written word into the midst of the nascent community in ways whose effects must have been electrifying. Words, theological ideas and arguments tumble forth, all geared to try to enable groups of very disparate people to live together and to learn what an ethic in the face of the 'impending crisis' might involve (1 Cor. 7.26; see Cupitt 2016). What Paul's letters bear witness to is that the messianic impulse is not just about the prophetic protest that points forward to a better world as it criticizes this one but also, alongside it, the patient, often painful, struggle to work out what it means in practice to embody that witness to the messianic age here and now.

Apocalypse, the revelation of hope

The previous chapter sketched the different ways in which we discovered the importance of apocalyptic ideas, their meaning and significance in the Book of Revelation. A chapter on the centrality of hope would be incomplete, however, without reference to *the* Apocalypse, which best summarizes the character of the theological imagination of the earliest Christian writings and the thoughts, persons and events to which they bore witness.

Apocalypse as 'unveiling' offers the rudiments of a critical language to question the status quo, and also the language of hope that instils a sense of dissatisfaction, and disturbs our complacency. Hope both goads and invites us into recognizing that a world in which creatures are exploited and made subservient to the desires of others does not and cannot constitute the true order of things and that something different is not just to be hoped for but worked for as well. The questioning of habits, values and social structures, together with the 'unmasking' of hidden powers and ideologies, is typical of what the Apocalypse offers and demonstrates how the Bible may contribute to the cultivation of a reflective life. The genius of early Christianity was not only to offer a horizon of hope but to ground that hope in concrete places of transformation, so that, to quote Paul's words, it could 'show a still more excellent way' (1 Cor. 12. 31). So, the New Testament Apocalypse has been such an important factor in discerning how and why we negotiate the ongoing creation of a critical space.

The distinguished philosopher Donald Davidson discusses metaphors and explains that they do their work by having an effect upon us: 'Joke or dream or metaphor can, like a picture or a bump on the head, make us appreciate some fact' (Davidson

2006, p. 222). The Apocalypse functions in exactly the same way. Notwithstanding the generations who have tried to decode its word-pictures to get at its essential meaning, it is the *effect* of this text that is all-important. Stirring us and making us think differently about ourselves and the world in myriad ways, this text paves the way for exploring an answer to the question 'so where do we go from here?' There is no prescription for that in the Book of Revelation. Indeed, when it comes to speaking about the future there is no blueprint, no utopian prescription. There is a reticence about laying out any kind of guide of the route to the New Jerusalem.

The gospel narratives of Jesus tell of the one who acted to make hope a reality. Paul's words are a series of essays in their time and place to those tiny groups dotted around the Eastern Mediterranean about what life may be like as communities of hope in their particular contexts. Together they offer different ways of exploring the consequences of the jolt to complacency offered by apocalypse, its horizon of hope and the unmasking of the injustice of this age. If the Apocalypse of John stirs us, the Gospel of John demands of us critical engagement with the reality of our present context.

How we learn from the jolt to our understanding offered by the effects of engaging with the Apocalypse is set out in the story of the life of Jesus, in which is revealed God's plan for humanity, as a recent interpretation of John 1.1–14 puts it (Ashton 2014, pp. 145–55). The plan turns out to be not an apocalypse of heaven but a narrative of a life lived and died, to borrow John Ashton's phrase, 'an apocalypse in reverse' (Ashton 2007, p. 329). Ernst Käsemann embraces both the Apocalypse to John and the Gospel of John in what he wrote about the revelatory character of narrative in the Gospel of John, which is a challenge to habit and tradition and which gives priority to apocalyptic vision:

> Many generations know of revelation only in preserved form and refuse to accept it in any other. Institutions, confessional movements and entire denominations rancorously strive over religious canned goods. They seriously imagine God would lose his identity if he were not caught and rendered concrete in this way, if he were not committed to inviolable theological formulas and thus become a calculable object in pious interchange. With these efforts grave-watchers of the sacred past calculate who Jesus is and must be, that is, the one who fits the religious concept or traditional program. The Johannine Christ reveals that the guardian of tradition makes himself judge of his Lord and protects himself from a new intervention of God. He no longer need fear any surprises from heaven, and on earth he defends the status quo of his convictions thus in effect is totally inaccessible. The Fourth Gospel unmasks such an understanding of revelation as the caricature of … discipleship … Let rebels and reformers take care lest the explosive power of its summons be smothered by what is merely edifying, lest organizational atrophy and manipulation allow the great theme of Scripture as gospel to be forgotten – that is, the exodus of the once imprisoned into the freedom of the children of God, and the presence of the rule of God over our life and earth. (2010, pp. 138–9)

The readers of John of Patmos's apocalyptic visions are not allowed to dream about millennial bliss without being brought face to face with the fact that a part in the New Jerusalem is linked with present behaviour and the need to prophesy before 'many peoples and nations and languages and kings' (Rev. 10.11). The tension is as real today as it was for those first Christians who wrestled with the longing that 'Thy kingdom come; thy will be done on earth as it is in heaven' and the demands of living in the midst of the old age.

Reflections

This chapter has concentrated on the 'horizon of hope' in the New Testament, and the priority, to use Blake's contrast, of 'Inspiration' over 'Memory'. It has also offered a textual witness to a pioneering demonstration of practical theology in the letters of Paul.

One of our earliest collaborations was on the theme of New Testament Theology and Practical Theology (Rowland and Bennett 2006). Its title, 'Action is the life of all' took some words written by the seventeenth-century theologian Gerrard Winstanley during a radical phase of his life: 'words and writings were all nothing, and must die, for action is the life of all, and if thou dost not act, thou dost nothing' ('A Watch-Word to the City of London, and the Army'). In that essay we saw Paul as a model of the kind of lived exegesis of the Bible we found in Winstanley's 'action' in 1649.

The often-quoted final paragraph of Albert Schweitzer's book *The Quest of the Historical Jesus*, written by a man who devoted his life to exploring the impact of that future hope on life and theology and who did more than any other twentieth-century scholar to explore the meaning of the eschatological convictions of the first Christians, has been fundamental for us.

> He comes to us as One unknown, without a name, as of old, by the lakeside. He came to those men who knew him not. He speaks to us the same words: 'Follow thou me!' and sets us to the tasks that He has to fulfil for our time. He commands. And to those who obey Him, whether they be wise or simple, he will reveal Himself in the toils, the conflicts, the sufferings, which they shall pass through in His fellowship, and as an ineffable mystery, they shall learn in their own experience Who He is. (Schweitzer 1931, p. 401)

There is a clear self-involving character to what he writes. Schweitzer wrestled with Jesus' eschatological message and its impact. Indeed, his life offers one example of a contemporary response to the call to those by the lakeside. Some words from the final chapter explicitly seek to explain the centrality of eschatology and self-involvement and to show how they are linked:

> Men feared that to admit the claims of eschatology would abolish the significance of His words for our time ... But in reality that which is eternal in the words of Jesus is due to the very fact that they are based on an eschatological worldview ... They are appropriate, therefore, to any world, for ... they raise the man who dares to meet the challenge, and does not turn and twist them into meaninglessness, above his world and his time ... So that he is fitted to be in his own world and in his own time, a simple channel of the power of Jesus.

(Schweitzer 1931, p. 400)

These important words were omitted from later editions but encapsulate something of central importance of eschatology for understanding Christian origins and the New Testament more generally.

There is a lack of prescriptiveness about what happens when the response is made to follow Jesus. It is *un*-scripted. In this respect Schweitzer, whether consciously or not, reflects an element of the Gospel of Mark where 'being on the way' (Mark 9.34; 10.32; Luke 9.51, 57; Myers 2008, p. 257) is the context for learning. It is less, therefore, about any doctrinal content and more about what unfolds. What is to be understood comes in the conflicts, the sufferings. It is in *that* context that he will be revealed. Apocalypse, therefore, comes through experience in the narrative humdrum of life 'on the way'. That existential dynamic mirrors what happened 'of old, by the lakeside', but it is *their own experience* that offers the context for learning. Concentrating on the Corinthian correspondence we can see how, for better or worse, Paul's experience confirms Schweitzer's words that Christ 'will reveal Himself in the toils, the conflicts, the sufferings, which they shall pass through in His fellowship, and as an ineffable mystery, they shall learn in their own experience Who He is'. It is a paradigm for *any* kind of theology.

3

Turning Points along the Way

Introduction

Conversion is a common human experience: common in that it frequently happens, and common in that it is something human beings share. How conversion happens differs from culture to culture and from person to person. In religious terms the word is often used to indicate a turning, often a sudden turning, to embrace a particular faith: 'he was converted at a Billy Graham rally in 1954'. Not always sudden, conversion may be a slow process, though to warrant the name the experience must have pushed a person across a threshold that brings them to a new place. They may return, but it is never quite to the same place:

> You shall not go down twice to the same river … You *can* go home again … so long as you understand that home is a place where you have never been. (Le Guin 1996, p. 52)

Conversion may occur outside religious faith altogether, or may occur *within* a religious faith. It is stories of the latter kind of conversion that we tell in this chapter.

The conversions or turning points we describe here relate directly to our understanding of the Bible. They demonstrate the close, and for us inevitable, entanglement of the text of life and the text of the Bible. The 'horizon of hope' and the finding of a critical space, themes of our last two chapters, run through these stories like lettering in a stick of rock.

Zoë

Changing strategy: feminist reading

> Wives be subject to your husbands, as is fitting in the Lord. (Col. 3.18)

> I permit no woman to teach or have authority over a man … (1 Tim. 2.12)

Until my late thirties these verses structured my understanding of marriage and of church life, of what it meant to be a human being made in the image of God in male or female mode. I saw their message as entirely consistent with the message of the whole Bible. I saw them as having a deep insight into the fundamental dynamics of relationships between men and women. I liked them.

And then the 'consensus' began to break down. It broke down on two fronts over the same period of time, leading me into both cognitive and emotional dissonance. My 'turning point' in relation to the Bible coincided with a turning point in my personal life and with a turning point in the life of the church of which I was a committed member. An entire edifice of language and practice, a house of being (see Heidegger 2000, p. 83), crumbled around me.

A new understanding of the Bible

A moment sticks out. One revolutionary Saturday evening in the vicarage I let the next day's roast brisket burn in the oven. Our curate, Mary Hayter, had proudly given me her first and newly published book, *The New Eve in Christ* (1987). This book was clearly an intervention into the debate raging in the Church of England about the ordination of women to diaconate and priesthood. Hayter argued that there are two different strands in the New Testament writings – the emancipatory one ('there is no longer male and female; for you are all one in Christ Jesus', Gal. 3.28) and the conservative one, as in the verses quoted above. She argued that the Christological strand – the one that came new in Christ – should take priority for Christians over the conventional morality as found in the so-called 'household codes': hence her title *The New Eve in Christ.*

Reading the book, I forgot the roasting beef. And it is no wonder. Because with that one insight, seen in a flash but tested and worked out over the years that followed, my world turned upside down. Some argue on prior theological grounds that we cannot make that move – that there has to be a consistent message in the Bible, not two voices – but once I had seen it there was no going back.

This (the different voices/strands) is a fundamental insight that I can trace through all my later wrestling with feminist and other theology. Itumeleng Mosala's book, *Biblical Hermeneutics and Black Theology in South Africa* (1989), took that further for me – not only might there be different strands but they might be struggling for the dominant, the hegemonic, voice in our text of the Bible. Ideological criticism can be found and explored *within* the Bible – in the genesis of the text itself (see Chapter 6).

The final possibility that my reading of feminist theology forced me to confront was that the biblical text itself might be the problem (Fontaine 1997). Women's experiences and voices are not evident in the pages of the Bible, and when they are found the women who are portrayed are often seen negatively. The Bible has been used as a tool of the oppression of women and to legitimate the dominance of men. The problem is at a much deeper, theological, level too as the images and language for God, and the actions ascribed to God, are predominantly male in character. The male, and stereotypically masculine attitudes, capacities and actions, are thus more highly valued and regarded as 'god-like'. It is this God whose omnipotence authorizes and guarantees the sacred text, and this God whose authorized interpreters are so often male, the justification for which is both biblical and also based on the very nature of God. Liberation theology privileges the voices of those who are not being heard, of the oppressed, but women's experience raises radical question marks over that story itself as well as the use we make of it.

A new understanding of life

As my understanding of the Bible underwent a sea-change so did my life.

The way I relate to men was substantially created by my father, a loving man who affirmed me deeply within the space he desired that I should inhabit. He created safety, 'a house of being', and he made the rules. His anger was unpredictable; he needed to be managed. Saying sorry always secured forgiveness. He did what he chose, and he was head of the household.

Such a view of men, and of God, later received legitimacy and reinforcement for me from a conservative evangelical reading of the Bible. Of course it is also true that I embraced, from the age of 16 when I joined a church, the reading of the Bible on such matters precisely because it fitted my experience, and the emotional and psychological needs shaped by my father. So I conceived of God for my first 20 years of being explicitly 'a Christian' (16 to around 36) as an essentially kind and loving, but sometimes, and not always predictably so, fierce and frightening, patriarch. God was at rock-bottom good and just. God offered a house of being, or a house of myths, outside of which was the outer darkness, the abyss, in which meaning and truth had been sucked into a vortex and there was no foothold. Crucially also God was at least infallibly if not inerrantly revealed in the Bible, and to lose that foothold was to descend into a cognitive and epistemological vortex parallel to and greatly reinforcing the emotional and spiritual vortex. There was a dynamic and nerve-racking interaction between personal experience and intellectual growth.

When I joined the youth group at my local church, and for the next 20 years, I was offered an alternative world, an alternative philosophy of life, and an alternative set of practices. But crucially this didn't really offer an alternative way of thinking about and relating to men, and therefore God.

He was still the patriarch, still not pleased when I stepped out of (his) line, still the provider of a house of being beyond which was the abyss.

Within this milieu my house of being was not only constructed implicitly by a man's temperament, not only constructed by the social *mores* at the time and in the context in which I dwelt, but constructed *explicitly* through a reading of the Bible, specifically the 'household codes' (as quoted at the beginning of the chapter). The men as leaders, the man as the head of the household, were given divine legitimation. This authority was authority legitimated by a conservative reading of the Bible on the roles of men and women, as well as being parasitic on a recognized, and in my case interiorized, cultural norm. And so my construction of 'manhood' was formed, and with it my construction of God. That construction was partial, deficient, and indeed dangerous, and it was by no means one that all men would own, but it was born out of my experience and out of the teaching about the Bible which I received.

This understanding of manhood was deconstructed in the midst of the debate about women's ordination, different patterns of gender relations in my working context, and theological study that raised questions about how we know what we know and what 'revelation' in the Bible might mean. For those for whom the Bible is 'the word of life' it is impossible to separate new understandings of the Bible from new understandings of life. *The New Eve in Christ* opened up a world of new vistas on both; and, inevitably as its title suggests, the possibility of a 'new' identity – though crucially an identity in some continuity with the past, including my 'pre-Christian' past and its humanist orientation.

A journey

These embryonic new understandings of the Bible and of life grew in the womb of my teaching. Feminist theology was the means through which I came to articulate them. Teaching in an Anglican theological college in the 1990s I came face to face in the classroom with the pain, conflict and hope of the intense debate about the ordination of women. At the same time, the context of an ecumenical federation of theological institutions brought into the classroom a diversity of histories and practices, of critiques and commitments. The encounter with feminist theology was a long-drawn-out 'turning point', and teaching, to adjust the metaphor, was the labour ward in which the one-time embryo was given birth.

Others' life-stories shaped mine: women deeply damaged psychologically and physically by the way their communities had used the Bible 'against' them, women for whom the Bible had been a refuge in the midst of such abuse, and men struggling to make sense of their role and identity. The very first class I taught on feminist theology comprised four men. The creative way in which they listened to women's voices, engaged with the analysis of Church and society as patriarchal, and were prepared to struggle with their own identity in the light of these things, has meant that I have always believed men could be feminists. A feminist is surely a person (woman or man) who accepts the understanding of society as patriarchal, believes this needs to be changed, and is committed to working for change. That women's experiences, expressed in women's terms, are essential to a feminist perspective does not mean only women may be feminists.

My feminist critique was forged and shaped in relation to the Bible in the long-running MA module I taught, *Feminist perspectives in pastoral theology*, which eventually formed the basis of a book (Bennett 2002). The first assignment task was always to choose a passage from the Bible and analyse it using a feminist methodology. In this, theory was subservient to first-hand imaginative engagement with the text. The address to the actual text in minute particulars took precedence over the theories behind a feminist interpretation. Or rather, the theories had to be discussed as they arose from the text, not the text used as a way of illustrating theories. The participants had to do their own work in relating what they had learned to a text, not just comment on other people's work. Does this pedagogical process itself say anything about my way of working with the Bible? I think so. The process made an attempt at democratization of educational method, and I wasn't afraid to include the Bible within that open process.

Addressing the Bible as the first item on the agenda of learning about feminist perspectives on pastoral theology was a decision I made at the start and never changed over 15 years. Why did I make it? One reason was external. Some of the earliest 'second wave' feminist theology came from the biblical scholars – Letty Russell, Elisabeth Schüssler Fiorenza, Phyllis Trible – or addressed the role of the Bible – Rosemary Radford Ruether (1983; 1985). There was an internal reason too. Having been nurtured in an open evangelical tradition it would not have occurred to me to start anywhere else. I saw the Bible both as the source of Christian belief and practice and as the root of the trouble. Dealing with it, as a central plank of my own learning and teaching, I soon found that almost everyone who came on the module also regarded the Bible as a well-spring of their Christianity, and that starting with a feminist critique of the Bible worked well across the traditions.

On the journey from the shock of the *New Eve*, to engagement in teaching feminist theology, my understanding of God and of gendered human relationships underwent a sea-change. It is impossible in this process to detach understanding of God from understanding of human relationships, as Daphne Hampson so rightly points out (1990). I had lived within a totalizing ideology in which cultural norms, divine legitimation and psychological dependency mutually reinforced each other. This seemingly impenetrable suit of armour was breached by two processes: naming my 'suit of armour' and in so doing naming alternative possibilities; and seeing in practice alternative ways of human relating and alternative ways of conceiving, addressing and relating to the Divine.

Without that ideological critique, that deconstruction of my relationship with the Bible, which was driven by the dissonances in my life-experience, I could have made no progress. But there was also reconstruction. Two constructive movements were already set in motion by the engagement with feminist theology.

First there was imagination. Schüssler Fiorenza's work,

especially in *But She Said* (1992), offered an invitation to imaginative engagement, and one that could be filled with the silent voices, even the non-existent names, of the women in the Bible stories. My students and I reimagined the stories as if told by the silent female characters – filling the right-hand pages of 'Bibles' printed only on the left with the voices not heard in the text. Thought-experiments gave contours and colours to C. S. Lewis's contention, quoted in Hampson, that 'A child who had been taught to pray to a Mother in Heaven would have a religious life radically different from that of a Christian child' (Lewis 1970, pp. 90–1). S/he would indeed. And Jo Ind's *Fat is a Spiritual Issue* (1993) showed me how that might be. Jo had been a member of the same church youth group as I had. Writing of her experience as a teenager with an eating disorder, and a somewhat distanced father who showed little warm emotion towards her, she says:

> In the presence of my heavenly father I felt more ashamed of my weakness, not less … When I saw God as masculine I saw the world as a hierarchical structure with the good people at the top and me, a compulsive eater, stuffing miserably at the bottom … When I was a child I saw a sticker on the back of a car saying 'Talk to God. She listens' … I pointed it out to my mother and we agreed that it was blasphemous … But when [as an adult] I considered what 'father' meant to me, a solution appeared in my mind. What if God were my heavenly mother? For surely God was both male and female and neither, because God is a mystery … When I imagined that God was my

> heavenly mother, the context in which I had an eating disorder changed. It is not an exaggeration to say the whole world became a different place.
>
> I realized that God was close, not distant. She was as close to me as I had been to my earthly mother in the womb … When I came to my heavenly mother and told her about my eating disorder I did not have to explain. I could rest in the presence of the one in whose image I was made. Worries about stretchmarks and thighs had a place – I pictured her as being on the round side herself … nothing I had experienced was alien to her. I rested in the love of one who knew. (p. 41)

Second there was correlation. Rosemary Radford Ruether used the term 'correlation' to show how the internal critique of religion conducted by feminist theologians could be correlated with the internal critique of their own religion by the Hebrew prophets and by Jesus. This set the work of critique within the biblical text itself. It was through Ruether's work as a liberationist feminist theologian that I found a place to stand within Christianity. Not to stand still, but more a resting place on the journey, fruitful for my ongoing faith and struggle with the Bible.

And a resting place

Rosemary Radford Ruether's idea of 'correlation' suggests that a liberationist-feminist reading of the Bible finds not that any strands in the Bible, even the prophets or Jesus, directly advocates a feminist critique, but that the contemporary feminist critique of contemporary Christianity can be 'correlated' with the prophetic critique in the prophetic books and in the gospels of the religion of their time (1985). Thus the Bible itself is foundational for making a critique of Christianity.

At the same time as the idea of 'correlation' gave me an interpretive framework for reading the Bible, a further move of Ruether's allowed me to set that biblical interpretation onto a wider theological canvas. In her debate with Daphne Hampson (1987) Ruether declined Hampson's invitation to admit that Christianity was irredeemably sexist (including its scriptures and its root language and imagery), and that only outside of Christianity was there any possibility of women and men having relationships of equality (Hampson 1990). Christianity, argued Ruether, is not primarily a historical religion but an eschatological faith. The possibility of critiquing both the religious status quo, and its anchorage in historical forms, texts and practices, is ever present in a faith that looks always towards God's calling to and promise of something better. The past, as the present, contains 'shiny bits' in the rubbish (Radford Ruether 1995, p. 53), but does not, as a 'concretized' whole, determine belief or practice, hope, memory or desire.

Thus a feminist liberationist position, which crucially included a way of reading history, theology and the Bible within an eschatological framework, allowed me a critical space within Christianity, which enabled me to move forward from the stultifying place I had come to.

Christopher

Transforming biblical exegesis: Brazil and liberation theology

The journeys to Brazil

As I was contemplating my first sabbatical leave at Jesus College after four years in post in 1983, a friend who had just returned from Bolivia questioned whether my plan to spend time in Germany and Israel best reflected my political interests: 'Why not Latin America?', he said. As I wrote at the time 'the experience of being in Brazil was more important than talking theology'.

I hoped that I would see liberation theology at the grass-roots at first hand and meet the liberation theologians who were involved in that way. Most memorable were the meetings with ordinary people, and, despite my linguistic limitations, seeing the extraordinary way they linked faith and life in the midst of the least promising of circumstances.

I was fortunate to capture a moment in Brazilian life where the Church had a unique opportunity which at that stage it grasped with both hands, and the fruits of the struggle in the 1980s have led to significant improvements for the poor in Brazil. What began to dawn on me in the light of my experience in Brazil was that life under a military dictatorship meant that the Church was the one institution that was not 'closed down' politically. Consequently it opened its doors to all who struggled for a better life for all, and so became an umbrella for a variety of people who were concerned about poverty, inequality and human rights, who would not previously have darkened the doors of a church. Instead, they found the Church and its representatives, particularly in the Archdiocese of São Paulo, but in many other places too, urban and rural, extending the hand of fellowship to be partners in the struggle, to quote the memorable words of the opening of *Gaudium et Spes*:

> the joys and the hopes, the griefs and the anxieties of the men [and women] of this age, especially those who are poor or in any way afflicted, these are the joys and hopes, the griefs and anxieties of the followers of Christ. Indeed, nothing genuinely human fails to raise an echo in their hearts. For theirs is a community composed of men [and women]. United in Christ, they are led by the Holy Spirit in their journey to the Kingdom of their Father and they have welcomed the news of salvation which is meant for every man [woman and child]. That is why this community realizes that it is truly linked with [hu]mankind and its history by the deepest of bonds.

'Life' or 'reality' is, if not more, as important a text as the text of Scripture itself. It represents another text to be studied alongside that contained between the covers of the Bible. This twofold aspect is well-brought-out by Carlos Mesters:

> the emphasis is not placed on the text's meaning in itself but rather on the meaning the text has for the people reading it. At the start the people tend to draw any and

> every sort of meaning, however well or ill founded, from the text … the common people are also eliminating the alleged 'neutrality' of scholarly exegesis … the common people are putting the Bible in its proper place, the place where God intended it to be. They are putting it in second place. Life takes first place! In so doing, the people are showing us the enormous importance of the Bible, and at the same time, its relative value – relative to life. (Mesters 1993, p. 14)

I recall two occasions shortly after I arrived in 1983. The first, which I have written about previously (Rowland 2007, p. 1), was my first Saturday in Brazil, appropriately May Day, when I spent the morning at a workshop taking place in a favela. Two professors of exegesis from the Pontifical University were there, leading a session on the Book of Revelation. Participants shared their experiences of witness, endurance, and tribulation stimulated by the words in Revelation 1.9. The message of hope from Revelation was one with which they all resonated. On that occasion relating everyday experience and the Bible there was a theology worked out not in the tutorial or seminar but in the midst of a life of struggle and injustice and where the insights of men and women, who found themselves caught up in the struggle, mattered.

The two professors, who became good friends thereafter, stressed how their lives had been transformed, as had their approach to the Bible, by participation with workers and how they approached the Bible with their questions in mind: if we have a struggle like this in our social setting, what must it have been like for the first Christians? They said how essential it was for them to understand the socio-political implications of texts, which would have passed them by if it hadn't been for the engagement with the poor and the workers whose experience was so different.

A couple of days later I visited another favela to meet community leaders, and we were welcomed into the home of a woman, who managed to make ends meet by cleaning for a rich family and then spent the rest of her life offering asylum for street children, either abandoned or orphaned. She welcomed me and my companion into her home, set out a table with the best crockery and then made wonderful Brazilian coffee. She offered me an example of how to create a space for human flourishing in the midst of the most unpromising situation. It was a sermon in action that will stay with me to my dying day. It is not surprising that there began a revolution in my heart as well as my intellect.

Engaging with the Bible in Brazil

My favourite example of liberationist exegesis and method comes from the *Parábolas de Hoje* (Parables of Today) series of slide sequences that relate stories told within the Basic Communities in São Paulo, Brazil to a parable of Jesus. I cannot read or listen to the story of the Lost Sheep in Matthew 18.12–14 without thinking of the slide sequence that introduces this. The story reflects the Brazil I first visited in 1983, which was then in the throes of a military dictatorship, and the Roman Catholic Church in a city like São Paulo offered a space for all those who sought to work for a different kind of politics. The story of the slide sequence would have been all too familiar. It concerns a young man who has been training for the priesthood and whose ordination to work with a local community is being prepared for. The night of the ordination comes, and the arrival of the bishop is awaited. He is delayed and a phone call is made asking what has happened to him. The answer comes back that he has gone to the police station to be with a trade union official who has been picked up by the police. The slide sequence ends, not with the bishop turning up late but with the bishop getting the union official released and escorting him back to his relieved family. We hear nothing about the gathered community nor whether the ordination ever happened! It is a brilliant analogy to Matthew 18.12–14:

> If a shepherd has a hundred sheep, and one of them has gone astray, does he not leave the ninety-nine on the mountains and go in search of the one that went astray? And if he finds it, truly I tell you, he rejoices over it more than over the ninety-nine that never went astray. So it is not the will of your Father in heaven that one of these little ones should be lost.

The work of the Church is to search unendingly for the needy. Church is not about preserving the ninety-nine sheep who at the moment are gathered together.

One meeting I often recall from a subsequent visit to Brazil was in Valença in Bahia in the North East of Brazil (Rowland 2013, pp. 133–48). There we visited an ecumenical education centre preparing popular education material for the base communities with a strong biblical slant. The method was essentially what I had learned from Carlos Mesters but put across in striking images that have been essential to my pedagogy ever since. Their emphasis on the Church as a 'down to earth' agency of the people appears on the front of *The Cambridge Companion to Liberation Theology*, which I edited. The material they produced was for illiterate people in rural areas. The heart of the images was the emphasis on the fact the first book that God wrote was life not the Bible.

The parish had been served by Salesian Fathers for the last 25 years. Their visits to an enormous parish were few (two or three times a year), which places enormous responsibility on lay people to organize the local community. They wanted to repeat the experience of popular education in São Paulo, as they believed that the work of the *comunidades eclesiais de base* (CEBs) only advanced where there was that popular education initiative. There were 20 pastoral agents, with an 'animator' in each area supported by executive teams with workers from the centre. They had six main areas of work: popular education, work with rural unions, political education, a theological correspondence course for animators, which involved basic literacy if needed, solidarity and human rights, and published material. The centre in Valença served anyone who needed it and was not just for the parish. They explicitly linked themselves with Carlos Mesters' work. I saw a programme put together to orientate missionaries coming to Brazil on ways of reading the Bible and the need to take *seriously* the realities of life in that context.

A sequence of posters explain and challenge the way of

being Church with a different emphasis on the Church as a down to earth phenomenon of the people rather than being about otherworldliness. Included in this explanatory process are reflections, including the question of leadership. They talked of the model of theological reflection with the Bible at the centre and the spokes of the wheel being the various kinds of participation and about experience. The wheel moves when the struggle is entered into. There was an emphasis on the importance of the life of the people and their context (Rowland 2013).

We went to a mass to mark the end of the month of biblical study on the role of women. At it there were many locally composed songs, sung with an intensity and fervour that was unforgettable. We were treated as honoured guests and at the offertory received gifts representing the labour and character of the local communities, which I still have. We introduced ourselves and I said a blessing over the bread. The confession consisted of the priest putting a dead plant and a live plant on the altar. On the dead one were put labels with words concerning that which individual members wanted to seek forgiveness, and on the live tree were cards saying justice, solidarity, love, truth and faith. At the homily members of the community were asked to say what they got out of their Bible study on women. All had enjoyed it, and several said that the male dominance in the Bible had been shown to have another side to it. At the end of the service we were surrounded by people who wanted to shake our hands and hug us and children who wanted me to speak English, which amused and fascinated them!

Back home from Brazil

I could never again be the theologian who stepped onto that Air France plane at the end of April 1983. Try as I may to pick up the threads of how I had been a scholar previously, the way of doing theology and biblical studies in which I had been brought up was gone for ever. One of the problems posed by my exposure to liberation theology is that it is about commitment rather than detachment, and so is something of a Trojan Horse – the intrusion of the interpreting subject into the scientific world of the academy. For the last 30 years with varying degrees of success I have attempted to square the circle by finding places to engage in the kind of work with the Bible that I saw going on in the CEBs of Brazil and seeking to emulate the intellectual endeavours of the committed exegetes that I met in 1983. What I discovered was that this kind of work does not translate into research and writing, which 'counts' in the academy. I found myself drawn to groups on the fringes of the mainstream Christian theological tradition whose positions and priorities in many ways anticipated liberation theology. It seemed then, and continues to do so, that there is a rich tradition, some of it completely unknown, which deserves a hearing. Most of it is far removed from the ancient historical study of the era of the origins of the New Testament, the prerequisite for the treatment of my subject in the academy.

At first sight, the impact of liberation theology on the centres of theological power has been small. Its reception into mainstream European theology, in particular biblical theology, has been lukewarm. If people ever say that liberation theology has failed, my response is to echo the word inscribed over Christopher Wren's tomb in St Paul's Cathedral, *circumspice*. Around us we can see the extraordinary impact of liberation theology on the action-reflection model of adult theological education. The place to look for liberation theology in these islands will not at least initially be in universities or colleges, but in grass roots groups, justice and peace groups, campaigns against the arms trade, Third World support groups and also in the many training courses that have espoused a pedagogy inspired by liberation theology.

A historical retrospect

What I learned in Brazil led to a journey into neglected byways of the Christian tradition to the priority of experience as stressed by Gerrard Winstanley (1609–76), who contrasts what tradesmen speak by experience of the things they have seen in God, and the 'hearsay preaching' of the learned clergy, and his suspicion of 'the literal knowledge of Scriptures of the Prophets and Apostles, and … the History thereof', without experience. Winstanley will have none of the attempt to create distance between text and reader, or doctrine and life. Objective, detached engagement with the Bible was anathema to him (Corns, Hughes and Loewenstein 2009, i.547–8). What is required is 'experimental knowledge', not abstract reflection on the Bible and the secondary application of it.

In my inaugural lecture at the University of Oxford in 1992, I tried to marry what I had learned from my study of apocalypticism with my experiences in Brazil. The title of the lecture ('Open Thy Mouth for the Dumb': A Task for the Exegete of Holy Scripture) was the quotation from the Book of Proverbs that Bonhoeffer used in the 1930s to describe the task of the Church in raising its voice on behalf of the Jews. In the lecture I outlined an approach to biblical exegesis which reflected similar contextual concerns to those enunciated by Bonhoeffer in his day. By a happy coincidence, the lecture was given at the beginning of Christian Aid Week. Christian Aid had been a regular feature of the life of the British Churches, and the context of much of my extra-curricular endeavours over the previous seven years.

1992 marked the centenary of the publication of Johannes Weiss's epoch-making book about Jesus' eschatological message. It enabled me to mark the central role of eschatology and apocalyptic in New Testament studies, and to mention another advocate of eschatology, Albert Schweitzer, who in his own time met the Stranger by the lake, to allude to the closing words of his famous book, *The Quest of the Historical Jesus*. He responded by leaving behind the distinguished career as a musician and academic to become a medical missionary. For him the Bible and life coincided (see above p. 54–5).

Finally, I referred to the presidential address of the German New Testament theologian, Ernst Käsemann, to the international New Testament society (*Societas Novi Testamenti Studiorum*). In it he emphasizes the link between history and exegesis and the way they

> exercise a function in the life of the Church and relate to the community in which Christians live. If, however, the one is abstracted from the other, not only is sacrifice

> offered on alien altars but the claim of the object we study and the service we might render are both alike misconceived'.

He then went on to say that 'were my work of no possible help to [Dom Helder Câmara, the radical Archbishop of Recife and Olinda in Brazil and advocate of liberation theology] in his troubles, I would not remain a New Testament scholar' (Käsemann 1973, p. 236).

A story I used at the start of my inaugural lecture in Oxford is one recorded in a collection of testimonies from the sixteenth century and concerns a chandler, Jacob, interrogated by a friar, Cornelis, in the presence of the recorder and clerk of the local court. During the discussion the chandler, Jacob, quoted the Book of Revelation in support of his views which provoked a heated response from his interrogator:

> 'What do you understand about St John's Apocalypse?' the friar asked the chandler. 'At what university did you study? At the loom, I suppose? For I understand that you were nothing but a poor weaver and chandler before you went around preaching and rebaptizing. I have attended the university of Louvain, and for long studied divinity, and yet I do not understand anything at all about St John's Apocalypse. This is a fact.' To which Jacob answered: 'Therefore Christ thanked his heavenly Father that he had revealed and made it known to babes and hid it from the wise of this world, as it is written in Matthew 11.25.' 'Exactly!' the friar replied, 'God has revealed it to the

weavers at the loom, to the cobblers on the bench, and to bellow-menders, lantern tinkers, scissors grinders, brass makers, thatchers and all sorts of riff-raff, and poor, filthy and lousy beggars. And to us ecclesiastics who have studied from our youth, night and day, God has concealed it.' (van Braght 1950, pp. 774–5)

Reflections

We both tell our stories in terms of a journey – in Christopher's case a geographical journey, in both cases a journey over time in which the circumstances of our lives are intertwined with our understanding of the Bible. The life story drives the story of our interpretation of the Bible, but the two cannot be neatly divided as our understanding of the Bible is in itself part of our life story.

One striking difference between our 'turning points' is that Christopher travelled to Brazil and Zoë stayed at home. At first glance Christopher's critical space was opened up by journeying to a strange place, and visiting people whose condition, priorities and practices were radically different from anything he had known before. Zoë's critical space was opened up within the town, the people, the university and the workplace that constituted her ordinary daily life. The view from elsewhere and the 'flipped' view from inside both furnish a critical perspective.

The role of the self in these stories has both differences and commonalities. Christopher saw that his mode of scholarship had omitted crucial commitments and practices that he was ready to embrace; Zoë saw that her inhabiting of a particular biblical hermeneutic was both contestable and destructive. The conversion in both cases was not primarily cognitive, though this aspect followed, but in the first instance affective and conative, involving the heart and the will.

On closer inspection there is more in common. The point is hinted at in the previous sentence; the conversions were not primarily cognitive. This is more immediately apparent in the case of Zoë's, given the roots in her relationship to her father, but, as the following chapter indicates, Christopher's journey to Brazil was also a pilgrimage of deepening self-understanding as well as the discovery of a theological framework and language to understand and speak about things that were deeply true about himself. Liberation theology offered a way of bringing together a self-involving engagement with the Bible with a recognition of the fundamental political character of Christian faith and the indispensability of commitment to human solidarity. It became a necessary means of negotiating a space within a professional world that had always seemed so alien from school onwards.

Both are stories of scaffolding and of catastrophe, of continuity and discontinuity. Our journeys of learning developed for much of the time within 'zones of proximal development', (Vygotsky 1978) moving out beyond what we already knew to new but contiguous experience and learning in engagement with friends, peers and communities – Christopher's trip to Brazil and Zoë's reading of a book, both at the suggestion of a friend, the base communities in Brazil, and the communities of learning in Cambridge. But our stories also involve 'catastrophe', an overturning, a turning upside down after which life would never be the same again, nor would our understanding of the Bible: 'I could never again be the theologian who stepped onto that Air France plane at the end of April 1983'; '[a]n entire edifice, a "house of being", crumbled around me'.

Both stories contain the seeds of the rejection of heteronomy in reading the Bible (see further Chapter 7). There is a democratization in the reading of the Bible found in liberation theology and in feminist theology and, as Christopher notes, in 'neglected byways of the Christian tradition'. These appealed to us as a way to hold on to and develop our most cherished beliefs and commitments – to human relating as the most important practice in life, to attention to the marginalized and hidden, and to resistance to the abuse of power (political, religious and personal).

We have belonged to communities of interpretation, but these have been communities where the space for theology, and the nature of what counts as theology, and crucially the interpretation of the Bible, have been strongly contested. So in 'turning' as we did we took sides and made commitments that have affected every part of our lives since.

4
Inescapable Struggles

This chapter approaches the autobiographical in a different way from the last, though in both we tell autobiographical stories. In Chapter 3 the stories were about how our understanding of the Bible and its use developed through encounter with new situations that challenged our old interpretations. Its subject matter was the contextually shaped processes of how our understanding and use of the Bible, our consciously held 'espoused theology', developed (Cameron et al. 2010).

In this chapter we use a different method to be self-reflexive about our use of the Bible. The Bible for both of us is in our bloodstream. We reflect on how that manifests itself, in an 'operant theology'. So in this chapter we tell two very different kinds of autobiographical story – one about death and loss, the other about isolation and struggle. In both cases the Bible operates as an integral part of our stories. We tell the stories, and in the process we reflect on *how*, de facto, the Bible is part of our story; we unearth our operant engagement with the Bible. And finally we begin to analyse and compare the quite different ways the Bible functions for each of us.

We are aware in such work of the need of an ethical contract with both ourselves and our readers. We have a duty of self-care, and we have an obligation to our readers to be clear about the function and status of autobiographical material. We concur with Heather Walton in her description of performance autoethnography: 'speaking from experience can be a staged act, an intervention' (Walton 2014, p. 7). *Mutatis mutandis* this is true of our written stories. They are genuine attempts to tell truthfully our history with the Bible, but what we 'put on the page' serves the specific function of displaying how our lives have interacted with the Bible.

Zoë's story is in two parts, comprising events separated by over 30 years. The first begins with a cameo, the second with a sermon.

Zoë

Thomas *1979*

Picture a man and a woman standing at the front of an audience of about 130 young people, most aged 14–18, some, the 'leaders', a little older. The room is a large classroom; it is in a boarding school in Hitchin; and the audience are ranged in a wide semi-circle several rows deep, like a kind of rainbow arc. This is an evangelical Christian holiday, with meetings each morning and evening for singing, talks (*kerygma* and *didache* – evangelism and teaching) and prayer. These young people have been together for about six days but it feels like an eternity. Many know each other from previous 'house parties'; some are new.

What has happened in the last few days is new to everyone. There is a kind of breathless and miserable waiting – I think.

I cannot say I know because I was the woman at the front, and that is how it feels as I remember.

We speak – my husband first. He is the overall leader of this house party, as he has been for years, but for the last few days he hasn't talked to many of the young people there, just to a few older friends. Then I speak. Our text was Psalm 16.

Protect me, O God, for in you I take refuge.
I say to the LORD, 'You are my Lord;
  I have no good apart from you.'
As for the holy ones in the land, they are the noble,
  in whom is all my delight.
Those who choose another god multiply their sorrows;
  their drink-offerings of blood I will not pour out
  or take their names upon my lips.
The LORD is my chosen portion and my cup;
  you hold my lot.
The boundary lines have fallen for me in pleasant places;
  I have a goodly heritage.
I bless the LORD who gives me counsel;
  in the night also my heart instructs me.
I keep the LORD always before me;
  because he is at my right hand, I shall not be moved.
Therefore my heart is glad, and my soul rejoices;
  my body also rests secure.
For you do not give me up to Sheol,
  or let your faithful one see the Pit.
You show me the path of life.

In your presence there is fullness of joy;
in your right hand are pleasures for evermore.

We speak about the man's illness the previous year. He had been ill for a long time and had nearly died. But he was not given up to Sheol, and our souls rejoiced as we had felt the close presence of the Lord, known ourselves to be faithful ones however imperfect, and found the path of life and of gratitude to God.

But now something else had happened. It had happened right here in Hitchin, on a CYFA (Church Youth Fellowships Association) house party, in the hallway entrance of the school, in a pram. A few days ago. Our baby son Thomas had died. Just gone. A cot death. During tea. From this tiny moment, this tiny child, has come an encompassing history, a stream widening to a river, widening to a delta. But on this day it was still the headwaters, a spring pushing out of the earth which no one on that house party could resist or push back into the earth.

This time our souls had descended into Sheol; we had seen the Pit. If there was a path of life here it was in death. And if in God's presence there was fullness of joy, it meant something different from what it had before. We hoped and believed Thomas was in the nearer presence of God – 'ye behold Him face to face'. And we testified that God was present to us in death as much as in restoration to life. This was true.

What did we think we were doing standing up in front of those young people and speaking about ourselves, about Thomas and about God? So indecently soon. Was it about teaching them, as we normally would do in that time-slot? Hardly. Was it about bearing testimony? Partly. To them, but also for ourselves. I know we needed to connect with all those people who had been there, witnessed what had happened, responded in a hundred different ways. Was it about gaining some control? I expect so.

So to bear testimony, to connect with the community, and to gain some control for ourselves, we used a psalm. We used a psalm that was already engraved on our hearts. A psalm written thousands of years ago in a totally different religious, social and geographical context, but which existentially connected directly to us and to our experience.

We used part of a psalm – selected because it began to give us a lever on an impossible situation. It was a means of containing the overwhelming feelings. This psalm held the loss of Thomas for us, as the loss of Thomas fed our interpretation of the Psalm. The interpretative moment was a live event – the process of connecting scripture with experience was happening *in vivo*. Scripture changed how we saw our experience and our experience changed how we saw scripture.

I said unhesitatingly 'part of *our* experience'. This was not a lone experience. This engagement with the Bible happened within a community of faith and interpretation – vividly physically so. Furthermore we were both parents of Thomas. How we were at that time – in respect of Christian faith and in the living out of this in the context of our experience on the house party – I cannot disentangle from the faith I had learned from my husband and, at the time, shared with him. So the context was shaped by the evangelical faith I inhabited with him, and that movement of evangelical faith to which the house party belonged, which had shaped us both. My 'use' of the Bible in reading this psalm, and then basing my 'talk' to the young people of the house party on it, was shaped by a faith that already grasped at reinforcement of a trust in God whatever happened. We already indwelt a form of Christianity whose 'house of being' was the goodness of God, and which drew on the psalms of the Hebrew Bible to express both lament and trust in God. So I read the psalm and saw comfort:

> The boundary lines have fallen for me in pleasant places;
> I have a goodly heritage.
> I bless the LORD who gives me counsel;
> in the night also my heart instructs me.
> I keep the LORD always before me;
> because he is at my right hand, I shall not be moved. (16.6–8)

And I saw within this general comfort a particular reference to the sorrow and fears experienced at night: 'in the night also my heart instructs me'.

I saw reference to our recent history – a reference that claimed or perhaps reinforced the sense that God had been with us through near-fatal illness:

> For you do not give me up to Sheol,
> or let your faithful one see the Pit. (16.10)

And then the big new move: I saw in the final verse

> You show me the path of life.
> In your presence there is fullness of joy; (16.11)

that Thomas was also with God, even though in his case the earthly outcome was not to be saved from death but to live in the nearer presence of God. I referred this verse, in my feelings at the time, to Thomas not to myself.

It is amazing for me to look back now and see how much that verse meant to me, since it is precisely from the point of Thomas's death that I find very difficult the idea that there is any comfort in thinking that we will see our loved ones in heaven. While these verses of Hebrew scripture presuppose exactly the opposite, many Christians absorb them automatically into a theology of resurrection in which we will be reunited with our loved ones. It seemed so blindingly obvious to me that babies don't need their nappies changing or breast-feeding in heaven. And such physical things were so much part of who Thomas was to me and who I was to him that I could see nothing about any future reunion in heaven that would even touch the loss I felt of him as an earthly human baby. Whatever I felt when reading those verses was about Thomas being safe from harm; it was not about 'I'll see him again one day'.

Our relationship to the Bible was very direct – the testimony of the Psalmist was taken as both a promise of God to us and as an articulation of our own testimony. But in our case testimony to what? I am not sure it was to the presence of God with us but I guess it was to an unshaken belief that what had happened to Thomas was held in God's hand – that Thomas was held in God's hand.

'Thomas sermon' 2010 – *31 years later*

Trinity Hall, Cambridge, 31 October 2010

John 11: the Raising of Lazarus

Carl Dreyer's great film '*Ordet*' or 'The Word' tells the story of the coming of resurrection to two families in a small Christian community in Denmark, torn apart by pain, division and death. In an utterly compelling final scene, Johannes, declaring himself to be Jesus Christ, and impelled by the faith a small child has in him, prays over the dead Inger and raises her to life. Through this miracle the two families are reconciled, and Inger's husband's faith is restored. Any of you who have seen the much more recent film about a Mennonite community, 'Silent Light', will recognize the resonances of a woman's resurrection, reconciliation, new life in the community and in individuals, and the faith of a child.

So there the six of us film-club members sat at the end of the film, silent in the awesome presence of what we had just seen on screen ... and someone said, 'The question that you who are Christians here have to face is do you believe in resurrection?'

The story from John's Gospel that we have heard tonight is quite definitely about resurrection. Resurrection that people believed in alright – but which had quite different effects on their various lives – in Martha and Mary's case drawing them into faith and into the story of Jesus' suffering and of his coming into new life; in the case of the chief priests, Pharisees and the council (later in the chapter) drawing them into planning Jesus' death – 'if we let him go on like this everyone will believe in him, and the Romans will come and destroy both the holy place and our nation' (John 11.48). Resurrection is disturbing – deeply disturbing of the status quo. In its place in John's Gospel the raising of Lazarus is a sign of the resurrection of Jesus which is about to happen, but it is also the last straw, the reason he is put to death as a disturber of the peace.

I have recently become a grandmother for the first time. My grandson was born seven weeks ago, and he is – of course – utterly beautiful. Two weeks ago he went to the fifth birthday party of a child who shares his names, who lives in the same town and is the son of some friends of ours. Now both have as their second forename 'Thomas' for a reason – both their mothers had brothers called Thomas, and both of them died – one when he was nine weeks old of cot death, the other when he was 21 years old of cancer.

> 'Lord, if you had been here my brother would not have died.' (John 11.32)

That is the first thing both Martha and Mary say to Jesus as soon as they see him: 'Lord, if you had been here my brother would not have died.'

Whatever else resurrection is, it is not an escape from the utterly terrible and painful realities of human life. The presence of God, or if you like, the presence of Jesus, are not talismans against death and suffering. The long complex walk towards healing and towards life in all its fullness, towards reconciliation in the nation and community, towards renewed love in families, towards personal faith and meaning in life – do not come without struggle and pain. In the two films the families and individuals faced and lived out anger, madness, separation, betrayal, and also love, faith, loyalty and tenderness. In our Bible story Lazarus, the sisters and their friends faced the same – the pain of Lazarus' illness, the fear and anger at Jesus' absence, the hopelessness – indeed Jesus himself wept as he was deeply caught up in this story of human pain and loss, so powerfully foreshadowing the agony he was to go through in his own story so soon afterwards, a story impelled forwards by his bringing life to Lazarus and joy to his sisters.

'Lord, if you had been here my brother would not have died.' Is it true that death implies the absence of God? When a baby or a 21-year-old dies does that imply that the devil has won, or that it's all absurd? That God is not there? That the hairs of our head are not numbered? That our Father does not see the fall of a sparrow?

I guess this is a pretty appropriate subject matter for the night on which we remember all those who have died. How does it happen – that new life, that reconciliation, that renewal of faith, that breaking in of something that leaves us gob-smacked, as we were at the end of the film, sitting there in stunned silence, and changes us for ever unless we suppress it and crucify it? How does God meet us even in death, so that we can be reconciled to the living and the dead, so that we are impelled to live life to its fullest, (even indeed if that means giving our lives in death as it did for Jesus and does for some people today?) How does God 'unbind us and let us go'?

Tragically, and in a way that reduces me to silence, just as I reached this bit in the sermon preparation I read a message from a friend telling me of a colleague whose wife of only a few months died an hour ago of cancer. I have read and re-read that last paragraph:

How does God meet us even in death, so that we can be reconciled to the living and the dead, so that we are impelled to live life to its fullest? ... How does God 'unbind us and let us go'?

It felt indecent to say anything, so I read and re-read the verses from our gospel story:

> Mary said: 'Lord, if you had been here my brother would not have died.' When Jesus saw her weeping, he was greatly disturbed in spirit and deeply moved. He said 'Where have you laid him?' They said to him, 'Lord, come and see.' Jesus began to weep. So the Jews said, 'See how he loved him!' But some of them said, 'Could not he who opened the eye of the blind man have kept this man from dying?' (John 11.32–37)

There is no answer. For 31 years since our Thomas died when he was nine weeks old I have asked and re-asked that question. I had come to content myself with the view that God has a kind of general providence that has the final plan in hand but the details are left to the way things just happen in nature. Anything else seemed indecent.

The birth of my first grandson changed all that …

That is not an answer – it's a testimony.

Preaching this sermon in Trinity Hall chapel I was no longer as I was the week Thomas died 31 years earlier, trying to understand my life by the Bible, but the opposite, trying to understand the Bible by life. The lectionary gave me the Bible passage; I saw my role as enabling some kind of understanding of that passage in the hearers, and some imaginative way to engage with it. In so doing I needed first to connect with it myself, to take full-on the gospel message of resurrection laid out in it, to test it out against the things I had experienced and witnessed, to see whether I could believe in it, what questions it posed, how it might come to life in the events of my life and the lives of others. The filmic portrayals of resurrection, the deaths of a friend and a stranger, and above all the death of our Thomas and the birth of my grandson, are the means by which the story of Lazarus as told in John 11 comes alive and has meaning. I interpret what I know less of by what I know more of. The Bible story is interpreted mediately by the immediacy of life.

Preaching has been a part of most of my adult life, as a Reader, in the Church of England, and I have always preached from the Bible. In my twenties and thirties I would preach in the standard Church of England 'open evangelical' way of the time, which was to teach the congregation to be understanding and mature Christians by means of an exposition of the Bible passage set.

What did that way of using the Bible say about the community that used it? That we valued the Bible in and of itself as an essential ingredient of what it meant to be a Christian, and as an indispensable aid for teaching and forming disciples. 'All scripture is inspired by God and is useful for teaching, for reproof, for correction, and for training in righteousness' (2 Tim. 3.16). That verse was ingrained in our hearts. Through the Bible we would learn how to be mature Christians, and we could help and teach others to be mature Christians. So the Bible would have something to say to our present lives, individually and as a community, and the very act of imbibing the Bible in this way would enable us to be more 'clothed in Christ'. The Bible would mediate Jesus Christ to us.

The change in the way I preached came with the events described in Chapter 3 – a departure from the 'house of authority' (Farley 1982, pp. 165–8). Personal history and the grim intractability of world events (my daughter was working in the Middle East at this time) pushed me away from the certainties of my earlier faith, which I could no longer honestly preach the way I had before. God was no longer unproblematically mediated by the Bible in the way I had experienced in 1979 as I spoke on Psalm 16. But I still preached. Indeed regular preaching, carrying with it the need to be both honest and responsible, became the liminal situation, the knife-edge, of testing whether I still could speak of God and of the gospel with integrity.

Now I didn't see the preacher's work as being to teach people, but to open their eyes. I was looking to awake imagination not obedience. I knew the Bible was a much richer treasure than I had ever realized. I also knew it was much more problematic than I had ever realized. So I started to pick on the bits in the passage that I didn't understand or felt were hard to stomach. I reckoned that addressing these might be interesting to people and awake their imaginations to engagement with God and with the Bible.

I have offered as an example of self-involving exegesis, or putting myself on the page, two occasions when I spoke publicly of the death of my son. In the second the story of Thomas's death became one way to get a grasp on the hope, the complexities and the contradictions we face in wrestling with the Christian preaching of resurrection in John 11. Understanding of the biblical text came by seeing it through the lens of life. On the earlier occasion it was the other way round, or almost. It was not so much that *understanding* of life came by seeing it through the lens of the text; it was less cerebral and more visceral than that. I was finding a way to live in the face of death and loss, and Psalm 16 enabled me to do so. This second way of 'putting ourselves on the page' is exemplified also in Christopher's story which now follows.

Life in Babylon

> Pharaonic oppression, deliverance, Sinai, and Canaan are still with us, powerful memories shaping our perceptions of the political world. The 'door of hope' is still open; things are not what they might be – even when what they might be isn't totally different from what they are. This is a central theme in Western thought, always present though elaborated in many different ways. We still believe, or many of us do, what the Exodus first taught, or what

it has commonly been taken to teach, about the meaning and possibility of politics and about its proper form:

- first, that wherever you live it is probably Egypt;
- second, that there is a better place, a world more attractive, a promised land;
- and third, that 'the way to the land is through the wilderness'. There is no way to get from here to there except by joining together and marching.

In these memorable words at the end of his book, *Exodus and Revolution* (1985, p. 149), Michael Walzer suggests that there are things about the Exodus story which resonate with the experience of most of us. 'Where one lives is probably Egypt' rang bells for me, but whereas Walzer points to Egypt, I found myself turning to the image of Babylon.

Throughout its history the Book of Daniel has been a happy hunting ground for those who would construct a map of the future of the world, but it is less these visions about the finitude of world empires and more the narrative context that is my particular concern. The stories tell of educated young men suddenly being transported from life in their home city, Jerusalem, to the strange, opulent, world of the court of the king of Babylon, and finding themselves at odds with the surrounding culture. Throughout the Bible, from the stories of the Exile to Babylon through to the dramatic vision of Babylon seated on the many-headed beast in the Book of Revelation, Babylon has represented being confronted by an alien set of values, cultural and political dislocation, and the necessity of negotiating a way of existing in that situation. It is the kind of disorientation with which a subaltern people has to learn to come to terms, as they find a way of coping and surviving, assuming, that is, that they do not accommodate themselves completely to their oppressors' culture.

Life in 'Babylon' was not easy. It is evoked in the opening verses of Psalm 137, an experience that has resonated with many down the ages:

> By the rivers of Babylon there we sat down and there we wept when we remembered Zion. On the willows there we hung up our harps. For there our captors asked us for songs, and our tormentors asked for mirth, saying, 'Sing us one of the songs of Zion!' How could we sing the LORD's song in a foreign land? (Ps. 137.1–4)

The Jerusalem elite, exiled to Babylon, appear to have found themselves on the fringes of the royal court, confronted with critical moments that threatened death, such as we find in the stories of Shadrach, Meshach and Abednego in the Burning Fiery Furnace and Daniel in the Lions' Den, according to both of which they were punished for their non-conformity (cf. Benn 2004). The tales of the miraculous deliverance of Daniel and his Jewish colleagues (Dan. 3 and 6), the humiliation and abject words of submission to God on the part of King Nebuchadnezzar (Dan. 4.34–5) and the magnanimity of Darius the Mede, who replaced Belshazzar king of Babylon (Dan. 6.26–27), cannot mask the fact that life for these Jewish exiles, despite the fact that they were received at the Babylonian court, was precarious in the extreme. They were constantly at the mercy of the capricious whim of an autocratic ruler (3.13), however sympathetic he might seem to be (6.14). But it was particularly the courtiers (3.8–12; 6.4), who appealed to 'the law of the Medes and Persians' for their own ends (6.15) to persecute Daniel. These are famous stories but it is a little remarked passage (Dan. 1.8–17) that has had special poignancy for me over the last 50 years.

In it we are told Daniel resolved that he would not eat the royal rations of food and wine served in Nebuchadnezzar's court and persuaded the palace master to allow him and his companions to eat vegetables and drink water. Despite that frugal diet they did not appear to have suffered, much to the relief of the palace master (Dan. 1.8–17). Daniel and his companions found themselves at odds with the lifestyle into which they had been so suddenly thrust, not least with regard to food, such an important part of life and social intercourse. Jews down the centuries have always been faced with the challenge that Daniel and his companions encountered, at odds as they were with their new culture, the consequence of which is brought out in these verses. Their experience with food was symptomatic of the variety of challenges, social, cultural and intellectual, which faced Daniel and other exiles as they sought to negotiate life in Babylon. Their struggle has continued to inspire me, throughout my 50 years living in Cambridge and Oxford.

Another biblical prophet, Jeremiah, had exhorted the exiles in Babylon not to go on hankering after Jerusalem, not to agonize about how to sing the Lord's song in a foreign land but engage with their context in Babylon (Jer. 29. 4–9).

Jeremiah had written to the exiles communicating to them the divine counsel, that they should settle, build houses, plant gardens and eat what they produced, marry and give in marriage, and seek the welfare of the city in which they were in exile, 'for in its welfare you will find your welfare' (Jer. 29.7; Bretherton 2010, pp. 189–99). What we read in the Book of Daniel is an example of such a response. There was no prescription given for resistance or survival. Sometimes it may have been a life of complete detachment, but more often than not it meant finding appropriate ways to live with integrity, whilst seeking the welfare of the city they inhabited; that was a crucial part of life in Babylon.

Daniel and his colleagues had 'knowledge and skill in every aspect of literature and wisdom' and 'insight into all visions and dreams' (Dan. 1.17). Their alien wisdom enabled an insight that the Babylonian seers and courtiers did not possess, and, according to the Book of Daniel, their advice was called on by successive kings. So, they were not merely parasites at the royal court but made a positive contribution to the understanding of politics, for those with ears to hear, that is, bearing as they did an uncomfortable message about the temporary nature of even the most sophisticated and apparently impregnable empire and the coming of a very different kind of polity. The apocalyptic wisdom of Daniel and his contemporaries was offered to those who would hear what would make for their peace, whether it was Nebuchadnezzar, albeit temporarily, learning humility (Dan. 4.33), the ephemeral nature of empire (Dan. 2) or Belshazzar discovering the price of his arrogance and that he had been weighed in the divine balance and found wanting (Dan. 5.27).

It is a widespread assumption in modern biblical scholarship that, as a result of their experience the Jewish exiles not only discovered how to carve out and to create in the midst of the constraints of their circumstances a safe space to sing the Lord's song in a strange land, but also how to reflect on how they had come to find themselves in this situation in the first place. The period of exile was *the* time when ancient traditions were collected, and their import for the situation of the Jewish people better understood. Also, the yearning for a better world was imbedded in Jewish life, when, in the words of one of Daniel's messianic visions, 'one like a human being came with the clouds of heaven [and] To him was given dominion and glory and kingship, that all peoples, nations, and languages should serve him' (Dan. 7.13–14).

Learning to live in Babylon has been a cornerstone of experience for many, Jews and Christians, down the centuries. It is something that is central to the kind of non-conformity that runs like a thread through the Bible, from the lonely ethical vigil of the prophets to the socially disruptive narratives of the gospels and the Book of Revelation and the admonitions of the New Testament letters which are the foundation of Christianity. Life in Babylon is a theme that was taken up in the New Testament. The author of 1 Peter addresses the Christians as 'exiles' as he writes from Babylon, probably a way of referring to Rome (1 Pet. 1.1; 5.13), and the visions of the Book of Revelation depict Babylon as an oppressive culture and contrasts it with Jerusalem, the future city of life. Unlike in Jeremiah, there is no instruction in John's prophecy to seek the welfare of the Babylon of his day. Instead, in John's vision Babylon's fall is hailed with uninhibited jubilation: 'Fallen, fallen is Babylon the great.' The only strategy is prophetic witness, with the consequences of so doing (Rev. 11.7). Both perspectives in tensions with each other are crucial to understanding the nature and pitfalls of life in Babylon.

In this context William Stringfellow's *An Ethic for Christians and Other Aliens in a Strange Land* (1973) rang so many bells with me when I first read it. It is an address to fellow-citizens to understand their nation biblically, rather than allow the United States of America, its culture and values to determine the way the Bible is read. At the heart of his method is this conviction that the Bible can assist one to understand a particular moment of time because it enables an enhanced vision of the reality 'encompassing all things as in a moment' (1973, p. 152). So, it is about a particular moment, not the totality of history. One contemplates one's own history in all its particularity utilizing the Bible to interpret that. There may then be opened up a glimmering of recognition of the demonic and dehumanizing alongside the power of the resurrection which is at work alongside it.

Stringfellow offered no neat answers and does not expect to go to the scriptures as if to a 'self-help' manual that will offer 'off the shelf' solutions. Nor is he interested in abstract principles or grand theories to apply to the situations in which we find ourselves: 'Biblical politics', he says, 'furnishes no answers to our questions, it is more a question of offering reorientation'. The ethics of biblical people concern events not moral propositions: 'precedent and parable, not propositions or principle' (1977, p. 24). There is no norm, no ideal, no grandiose principle from which hypothetical, preconceived or carefully worked out answers can be derived because there are no disincarnate issues.

Taking seriously the particularity of one's context with all its flaws and its potential to manifest the signs of resurrection and the new heaven and earth means 'staying with' that situation, accepting being part of a context, subject (though not obedient) to the principalities and powers. That is a way of looking at things which so resonated with both my own situation and the role that the Bible has played in helping me get my bearings in it.

Not surprisingly, given the title, *An Ethic for Christians and Other Aliens in a Strange Land*, Stringfellow turns to the Book of Revelation, whose contrast between Jerusalem and Babylon offers an interpretative key to understand the cosmos under God. Whereas Babylon is a description of every city, an allegory of the condition of death (p. 49), Jerusalem is the city of salvation … The community of reconciliation, sanity, freedom, peace (p. 34), 'a prophetic society' (p. 52). The 'confessing' Church is 'spontaneous; episodic; radically ecumenical; irregular in polity; zealous in living; extemporaneous in action; conscientious; meek and poor' (p. 122). As important is that the 'marks of Jerusalem' may appear anywhere, however momentarily, and are not tied to the churches.

Like his ancient predecessor Tyconius, Stringfellow sees the book as a kind of lens through which one might see one's own situation. The Book of Revelation is apocalypse not so much as the cataclysmic destruction of the world, but as the means of insight or revelation. Apocalypse is the means whereby one gains insight into the fallenness of the particular historical situation and the powers that confront one, whereas eschaton is the hope that offers a different perspective.

What is required is the cultivation of a counter-culture. Indeed, in *Ethic* Stringfellow poses the questions 'How can we act humanly amidst the fall?' and 'How can we sing the LORD's song in a strange land?' (Ps. 137.4), and answers 'I hear that in the Book of Revelation's response to the question posed in this Psalm' (p. 21). There is a powerful tradition within the Bible of the notion of exile, a situation in which one might enter, literally or spiritually, to see things differently. That may include those in the corridors of power as well as on the margins, 'by the waters of Babylon'. In the Book of Daniel we find a member of the Jewish elite, not sitting by the waters of Babylon playing his harp, but in the palace of King Nebuchadnezzar, struggling to work out some kind of way of life in which he as an alien in a strange land can live and work in this sort of context.

Stringfellow's writing engaged me and prompted me to think about how it is I should live and work in the Babylon in which I was situated; exploring all those grey areas, the limits of compromise, what to protest about and what to keep quiet about, how to act prophetically, recognizing that 'the issue of biblical ethics is not expressed in vain efforts to divine the will of God in this or that particular situation' (1973, p. 151). Unlike Daniel and his colleagues in Babylon who were forced to be there, for many of us life in 'Babylon' and 'singing the

Lord's song in a strange land' have bourne in on us as the result of experience in places we have chosen to be. Coming to terms with the context above all else has been a long and painful process of learning to carve out space to 'sing the Lord's song in a strange land'.

As the letters to the seven churches indicate, who is 'in' and who is 'out' is not at all clear. Those who are most confident (the Laodicaeans) turn out to be the least included. Confessing the name and being part of an ecclesial community is not what counts (cf. Matt. 7.21–23); it is whether one has worshipped the beast and drunk deep of the fornication of Babylon. Confession and membership of a specific religious group is less important than non-conformity with the mores of the beasts and Babylon. The Book of Revelation offers a warning that what passes for civilization is deeply flawed. Jürgen Moltmann's words are apt, 'Peace with God means conflict with the world, for the goad of the promised future stabs inexorably into the flesh of every unfulfilled present' (2002, p. 21).

To return to Michael Walzer's words quoted at the start, the still open 'door of hope' and 'things are not what they might be' are fundamental also to Christian identity. As Ernst Käsemann, who suffered his tragedies, personal, professional, national and political, has put it, 'no one remains human who has given no room to death or failure in one's account book, who is not ready with Abraham and Israel to join exodus from the familiar world of Chaldea or Egypt. Biblical apocalyptic reminds us of this' (2010, p. 5). How one lives with apocalyptic hope when still in the desert or Babylon requires a biblically informed discernment to explore how far the messianic age may inform the welfare of Babylon.

In conclusion I offer an anecdote from my recent experience which encapsulates my alienated existence in Babylon. After preaching a sermon on life in Babylon in a college chapel I was asked by the man presiding at dinner, who had heard the sermon, 'Where is Babylon today?' I assumed that he was picking up the thread of the sermon that had dwelt on the figurative power of Babylon in religion and literature and its impact on contemporary Christians, so I answered in the spirit of my sermon. Only later did the penny drop, and it became clear that I had completely misunderstood him, when I was asked the same question by someone else but put more precisely in the form 'where was Babylon and are there remains of it today?' It was an issue that had never occurred to me when I was preparing the sermon and to be honest I didn't know precisely, muttering something about contemporary Iraq (correct). But the questions, and my lack of competence to understand and answer, says a lot about the way I naturally read the Bible and what is most important in understanding its contents – and that need not include ancient historical and archaeological information, which is interesting but not necessary. Second time round I did manage to respond: 'It is not the stones of Babylon about which I was speaking in the sermon but what has been made of the figure that was my concern.' But in that question surely lies the heart of my intellectual problem with much contemporary academic study of the Bible.

Reflections

The accounts in this chapter tell stories that span most of our adult lives. They are not 'critical incidents' offered for reflection, but lifetime journeys. Comparing on a larger canvas the ways in which the Bible functions for us, and interrogating these critically, will be the task of Chapters 7 and 8. Here we note some initial similarities and differences in the personal stories, the self-involving exegesis, we have offered in this chapter.

A fundamental point of difference and comparison is between reading life from the text or the text from life. In Christopher's story of life in Babylon, and in Zoë's story of the death of Thomas in 1979, we are both interpreting life from the Bible. This is in neither case a piece of deliberate exegesis but a way of living that included the Bible as the bedrock of the understanding of our lives. For Zoë in 1979 it was the common language of the community, the language she had got used to using, which both articulated and itself produced a deep sense of trust in God, that the last and final power is good. For Christopher his way of indwelling the Babylon texts (or they indwelling him) is not part of a communal language but is individual, lonely and counter-cultural.

Zoë's sermon in 2010 demonstrates a quite different approach, in which the problematic but enticing biblical text is explicated in a process of deliberate thought. Understanding what this story of the resurrection of Lazarus 2000 years ago might mean is explored by means of things in life which are known to the preacher and hearers. Here the Bible text is the unknown and alien, and life is the known through which we can enter the text. Differences in how the Bible and life are related not only show up between different people, but within one person at different stages of their life, and indeed in one person at the same time.

5
Companions on the Road

Part of any intellectual engagement that is critical is finding appropriate alternative perspectives to bring fresh understanding of a situation. In this chapter we explore the possibility that alternative perspectives might be offered by a historical figure. These perspectives have opened up for us a critical space for understanding the Bible, life, and crucially also the modes in which we might explore the connections between life and the Bible.

William Blake and John Ruskin have been two such figures in our lives and work, inviting us into imaginative, playful, and deeply serious engagement with both the Bible and life. The *ways* in which they saw connections between the Bible and life have been as important to us as the content of their vision. In this chapter we seek to demonstrate how grappling with Blake's and Ruskin's work has profoundly influenced our own journeys with the Bible, and through this to illustrate how the engagement with the life and work of a historical figure might bring an alternative perspective and fresh understanding.

Zoë

John Ruskin

John Ruskin (1819–1900) was a nineteenth-century public figure, art critic and social critic, whose life spanned the Victorian age (Hilton 2002). The Bible was in his bloodstream; he learned it at his mother's knee, reciting two chapters a day, starting with Genesis 1 and reading every chapter till he got to Revelation 22, and then back to Genesis 1 again, a continuous wheel of reading (Cook and Wedderburn 1903–12, 35.40–43). He read the Bible every day throughout his life, often in Greek, often in medieval copies he owned, and often scribbling notes on the pages. These notes, together with his dairy entries, reveal a man for whom the Bible was in his heart and soul. It stayed with him and he with it through periods of deep doubt and personal anguish, becoming to him a kind of critical friend to wrestle with in private, and an overflowing treasure to pour out into his public work – his lectures, his letters and his books. His most famous work of social criticism, published initially in 1860, is *Unto This Last*. The title is taken from the King James Version of the parable of the labourers in the vineyard in Matthew 20.1–14 ('take that thine is, and go thy way: I will give unto this last, even as unto thee'), and the work is soaked in Ruskin's understanding of the Bible as a call to live humanely in response to Jesus' teaching under the fatherly love of God for all (Wilmer 1985).

I became interested in Ruskin's work initially quite independently of my interest in the Bible. Visiting the home of his later years, Brantwood on Lake Coniston, I was overwhelmed by the story of a man who, in his later life, poured himself out in the struggle against the pitiless and unrelenting machine of Victorian capitalism. I was drawn in by the personal tragedies of his life (unfulfilled love and terrifying episodes of psychotic disturbance) and by the idiosyncratic ways in which he saw things and invited others to share the same view.

> [T]he greatest thing a human soul ever does in this world is to see something, and tell what it saw in a plain way. Hundreds of people can talk for one who can think, but thousands can think for one who can see. To see clearly is poetry, prophecy, and religion, all in one. (Cook and Wedderburn 1903–12, 5.333)

When the university I work for took Ruskin's name (Anglia Ruskin University) I decided to investigate whether he had anything to offer to theology and to practical theology in particular. He did (Bennett 2008; 2011).

My engagement with Ruskin and his relationship with the Bible has done two fundamental things for me. First, he has offered me a critical place to stand, outside my own context. Working with the public and private texts in which John Ruskin in the nineteenth century reveals his way of using the Bible (he reveals it more than expounds or discusses it) I have been given a fresh perspective on contemporary ways of understanding the Bible, including my own. Second, he has offered me companionship. His doubts, his history of faith, and the development of his relationship with the Bible are not my own. But they are analogous. They not only give me a critical space from which to understand, but they give me inspiration and encouragement. I admire this man who passed through the deep waters of the Victorian 'crisis of faith', and the deeper waters of the entanglements of emotional response to the Bible with the complex love of the two significant women in his life, and through it all he holds his integrity – never does he take the easy route of denying his doubts, and never does he take the easy alternative of casting aside his love for the Bible. I admire him, and I take courage from him.

Ruskin's engagement with the Bible became the focus of my research, and a highlight of this process was working with a medieval Gospel Lectionary that Ruskin had annotated on almost every one of its 155 double-sided pages (Egerton 3046, Evangelistarium, British Library). Sitting in the British Library Manuscripts Reading Room looking at that lectionary I saw the Bible in a living form I had not seen before, let alone handled. An eleventh-century manuscript: passages from the Bible running together from one to another on the page, and flowing Greek minuscule script, in two columns, impossible at first sight to tell where a given word ended, let alone a sentence or a gospel passage. And then at the bottom of each page was Ruskin's scrawling Victorian handwriting – comments assigned to verses, and even a cross at the left to denote a new gospel passage, that cross that blots itself on the facing page when he shuts the lectionary the day of his beloved Rose's death. He feels free to comment, to 'deface' this ancient manuscript, to let his soul respond to beautiful gold lettering and idiosyncracies of translation; free to ask questions, to articulate his disgust, his delight, his doubt, and the narrative of his struggle to understand; free to hear and note on the manuscript in ink the resonances between the biblical text and contemporary life. The symbiosis between the Bible and his own life appears in physical form here; the way Ruskin treated this manuscript is analogous to the way he treated the meaning and message that the words on the page offered. It shows a man so utterly at home in the text of the Bible that he could afford to question it, even be contemptuous, without losing his relationship with it. Something he wrote in an open letter illustrates the point perfectly:

> My good wiseacre readers, I know as many flaws in the Book of Genesis as the best of you, but I knew the book before I knew its flaws, while you know the flaws, and never have known the book, nor can know it. (Cook and Wedderburn 1903–12, 28.85)

The characteristics of Ruskin's biblical interpretation are consistent across his private and public writings (Bennett 2013). Some illustrate his fundamental commitments: a partiality for justice and servanthood as the heart of the gospel, a preference for practical obedience, a dislike of religious exclusivity and arrogance, and a suspicion of the obscure, otherworldly, eschatological and 'mystic'. Others indicate his method of reading and his approach to what he reads. He has an interrogative approach, always asking questions – why on earth are we told the name of the servant of the high priest whose ear was cut off? Why does the centurion think Jesus' cry on the cross proves he is the Son of God? 'Well questioned Jude!' (Egerton 3046 43V; John 14.22). He has a great capacity to live with doubt and uncertainty:

> [M]y very first principle in Bible reading is neither to want to *bring* out anything – nor to be *afraid* of *finding* out anything; and only to make sure that whatever I read, I either *do* – or *don't* understand … all depends on taking [the words] precisely in their accurate & entire meaning: then, if we understand them on these terms, all is well; if, on those terms they appear inexplicable, mark the text as a short one – clearly – with the chalk – 'That's a locked door' – Well, it would be odd if all doors were open at once – go on to another, and we shall perhaps find that one open when we come back. (Burd 1969, p. 156)

He has a deep interest in his own reading history: 'After all, the more I think the more puzzled I become – I suppose this was the way I lost understanding of the words before' (Ruskin Foundation MS 11, f. 107).

Finally, and of most interest here, is his way of seeing the text of the Bible and the text of life in an immediate analogous relationship, using the one to invite understanding and interpretation of the other. He sees the text of the Bible and the text of contemporary life in an immediate juxtaposition that sparks the imagination.

He reads the Bible and reads the 'signs of the times', holding both in his head and heart, and understanding the one through the other – the blood money for Judas' betrayal, which the chief priests will not put in the treasury, as the 'blood money' of Victorian capitalism: 'Our priests don't even warn our Chancellor of the Exchequer of such unlawfulness' (Egerton 65R; Matt. 27.6); the counterfeit counterpart of the good shepherd as the Bishops of his own time – 'Did he ever in his life see a wolf coming, and debate with himself whether he should fight or fly? – or is not rather his whole life one headlong hireling's flight without so much as turning his head to see what manner of beasts they are that follow? … How many wolves does he know in Peterborough – how many sheep? … what bites can he show the scars of?' (Cook and Wedderburn 1903–12, 28.242–3; John 10.12) – the smoke of the factories as the smoke of the Apocalypse 'and this smoke, which hides the sun and chokes the sky – this Egyptian darkness that may be felt – manufactured by you, singular modern children of Israel, that you may have *no* light in your dwellings, is none the fairer, because cast forth by the furnaces in which you forge your weapons of war' (Cook and Wedderburn 1903–12, 27.207).

This hermeneutic of immediacy, though it is rhetorical rather than historical-critical, is no proof-texting. It is the sharp insight of an engaged heart, which brings together texts, images, beliefs and commitments; it flows from an imagination stirred, which seeks to stir in turn the imaginations of others – and galvanize them into action.

When it comes to his own personal life Ruskin is, however,

more reticent. There is one striking example in the Lectionary notes where he simply doesn't see the connection between his own life and what is happening in the text – a failure (of nerve?) in the hermeneutic of immediacy. On 24 May 1875 he is in the middle of reading the story of Jairus's daughter and the woman with the haemorrhage (Luke 8.41–56). At this point Rose is dangerously ill. She was a young woman whom he had met as a child and fallen in love with when she was 'about 12 years old' (42). She was now 'dying' (42). In all the time he had known Rose 'her father and mother' (55) had constituted a complex mixture of his access to Rose and his debarring from her close presence. For years Rose's parents had 'spent all [they] had on physicians' (even if not financially in this case) 'and no one could cure her'. Rose's anorexic condition would have probably meant she would no longer have menstrual bleeding, and here is a text about an excess of menstrual blood (43), about a mother and a father and the giving of food (55). The two related stories and Ruskin's immediate and desperate life-concerns intertwine in the imagination of a reader, and provide just the sort of breeding ground for analogies, resonances and comparisons which were Ruskin's normal biblical reading strategy. But here he does not touch it; '*[s]ometimes – tell –sometimes don't tell – why*' he writes cryptically in reference to the injunction in verse 56 to tell no one what had happened.

Four days later, having heard of Rose's death on the 25th, he returns to that fateful day's page of Bible reading and, noting the blotting of the cross on the opposite page, writes: 'By *Fors* [here 'fate'] thus blotted with a double cross. I underline the former writing.' Rose, whose nickname for him was St Crumpet and who herself became in his imagination St Ursula, his 'favourite saint', had died. Now Ruskin inserts himself obliquely into the text of his marginal notes, and via this mediated route into the biblical text itself.

So Ruskin's relationship with the text of the Bible and the text of life, and his understanding of the connections between them, was actually both complex and nuanced, and inevitably not wholly consistent. Consistency was not a virtue Ruskin prized as a means to grappling with the truth:

> Mostly, matters of any consequence are three-sided, or four-sided, or polygonal; and the trotting round a polygon is severe work for people in any way stiff in their opinions. For myself, I am never satisfied that I have handled a subject properly till I have contradicted myself at least three times ... (Cook and Wedderburn 1903–12, 16.187)

The matter, however, is made even more complex, but more exciting for a practical theologian, in that in Ruskin's work one can see at least four 'texts' opening up. Beyond his private grasp of the connections between the biblical writings and the world in which he lived, Ruskin communicated his understanding of the first two texts, the text of the Bible and the text of life, in an outpouring of lectures, letters, and books. He externalized his thoughts and feelings, not artlessly, but in a way carefully and rhetorically crafted for impact. He intended that his words should do work in the public realm, and to that end he produced texts. Without such texts the 'human soul' may 'see something' but fail to 'tell what it saw in a plain way'.

From this a fourth text flowed seamlessly – the 'text' of deeds and actions. Ruskin believed that the heart of Christianity was the work of justice. In his private diary wrestlings with Paul's letters to the Romans and to the Galatians, as he works out his adult faith, over and over again he seeks to demonstrate that the word δικαιοσυνη and its cognates should be translated by the English word 'justice' rather than the word 'righteousness' (for example, Ruskin Foundation MS 11, f. 287, where he describes injustice as 'the great comprehensive Crime of crimes') – emphasizing the work of God and the work of the human community under a compassionate Father.

> You have – in the beginning of the New Testament – and at the end of it – two great teachings about the Kingdom, Both by Christ ... The first words are Matthew 5.3 – the last, Revelation 22.14–17 – giving (taken together) – the full blessing – first the subduing of the heart to obedience – then the fulfilment of obedience – then the Reward of obedience ... obedience by *action* ... When first however you begin to see how throughout the Bible Deeds are the test, and not words nor Creeds – there comes a terrible feeling over some minds as if they could never do enough ... [But] ... [a]s soon as people begin to work for Christ really – they find it just like working for their father in his garden. They never need to be afraid of not doing enough to please him – sometimes they may not do quite

> as much as they should – but all that He'll say will be, 'Well – my dear, I think you might have dug a little further this morning – but never mind – go and get your dinner – and I'll do this bit for you.' (Burd 1969, pp. 133–5)

The founding of The Guild of St George, whose Companions still today pledge money, land and work to build a better society, was one of his more enduring idiosyncratic schemes. His legacy was profound, inspiring Gandhi, Martin Luther King, and the early members of the Labour Party among others, and still spawning work in, for example, education, care of the environment, and social critique – what Stuart Eagles following James Sherburne calls Ruskin's 'strangely refracted influence' (Eagles 2011, p. 1).

Ruskin's life and work therefore display four texts: the texts of the Bible and of contemporary life, the reflective text in which what is seen is told, and the performed text, in which what is seen and told is acted upon, into which actions others are invited and by which they are inspired. It is impossible, though many would wish to do it, to detach the Bible, in his soul and on the pages he read every day, from Ruskin's life work. In him the four texts are inextricably interdependent.

In looking at how Ruskin lived and worked with the Bible I have found an inspiration to pursue the tasks of practical theology, and an analogy to my own ways of working which offer a critical space. I have found a courageous companion, whose deepest and most problematic relationships were entangled with the Bible (his mother and Rose) and whose public intellectual context threw personal doubt on the Bible

– 'If only the Geologists would let me alone, I could do very well, but those dreadful Hammers! I hear the clink of them at the end of every cadence of the Bible verses' (Cook and Wedderburn 1903–12, 36.115) – but who remained in critical friendship, reading it daily and responding to it, in marginal notes, in public lectures and books, and in the disposition of his wealth and quite literally his health. 'THERE IS NO WEALTH BUT LIFE' (Cook and Wedderburn 1903–12, 17.105).

Christopher

William Blake

A decade ago I was invited by one of my graduate students to share in a complete reading of William Blake's 'Jerusalem'. A group of 12 of us attended the event, among them Philip Pullman, a Blake admirer. Each member of the group was asked to share in turn their experience of Blake and his work. I found myself blurting out the words, 'Blake has taught me to read the Bible.' I had never articulated it like that before, but since then I have often recollected that off-the-cuff comment. I had never thought in that way before. I have reflected on the truth of that statement and come to see that Blake (as in much else in my intellectual endeavour) has been an important catalyst for my thoughts and understanding (Rowland 2010).

In trying to articulate what it is that Blake has taught me, I have started with this because the words 'Blake taught me' suggest a direct impact rather than a detached engagement with someone's words. There's always a sense when engaging with any of Blake's works that more is going on than a mere encounter with words or images. It is what is constitutive of what is 'more' that is one of the most important aspects of Blake's works, indeed, is the way he relates to pedagogy. I am not claiming some mystical experience with Blake in which Blake taught me. Rather, akin in some ways to the way Blake internalized Milton's genius, I have found that how I have engaged with Blake is less via conventional exegesis and more by a long process of internalization of the intellectual energy in his work. Blake does get inside one and reshapes the way one reads, views and looks at the world, and for that matter God. Thus, when reading the opening of *The Marriage of Heaven and Hell* for the first time after several years, it came home to me what a brilliant encapsulation it is of the way Blake takes one from the paths of 'ease' to the 'wilderness' as he shares the exuberance of the 'devils' and liberation from the priggish and narrow-minded 'angels' with their religion of 'thou shalt nots', which I've internalized for a lifetime. Blake has shown me a way of not being tyrannized by the Bible while at the same time being inspired by it.

What I find in Blake's work is a clear grasp of the shortcomings of the Bible, in both its contents and its effects in human history, while there is also a clear recognition of the inspiration that it offers. Blake was a true modern in his critique of the Bible but inherited the pre-modern knowledge of and affection for it. I saw Blake delighting in the Bible, considering that no text however revered should be placed on a pedestal and take the place of the patient and necessary task of learning to relate with others, and indeed using that revered text in imaginative ways. He stressed the importance of Inspiration and the priority it must take over Memory, and resisted resort to biblical prescriptions. In words that immediately precede England's unofficial national anthem he writes of the time when 'professedly Inspired Men [sic] will hold their proper rank, & the Daughters of Memory shall become the Daughters of Inspiration' (*Milton A Poem* Preface; E95). Blake probably learned from John Milton that inspiration was not 'to be obtain'd by the invocation of Dame Memory and her Siren daughters, but by devout prayer to that eternall Spirit' (*Reason of Church Government*, Preface to Book II).

The prior enriching by the Spirit seems to anticipate Blake's subordination of reason to inspiration or imagination:

> Why is the Bible more Entertaining & Instructive than any other book. Is it not because they are addressed to the Imagination which is Spiritual Sensation & but mediately to the Understanding or Reason. (Letter to Trusler 1799, E703)

For Blake the Bible is less a text to be interpreted but contains words that have an effect in whatever form of engagement one has with it. Anthony Thiselton, too, seems to be suggesting that there may be other ways of interpreting texts which may lead to a better understanding when he writes: 'the biblical texts function with the greatest integrity and coherence with their directedness when they function (where appropriate) as illocutionary acts of address, promise, commission, decree, praise, celebration, pardon, liberation and authorization' (Thiselton 1992, p. 616). But if we are 'self-involving' we also need to be self-critical. What is needed is the casting off of what Blake terms 'selfhood'. What seems to come across in the final pages of *Jerusalem* is that it is not just prophetic endeavour that matters but how to avoid the endeavour ending up a massive ego-trip.

For all the extraordinary inventiveness, learning, and wide-ranging scholarship that make up contemporary biblical studies, it is quite possible for a biblical scholar to miss the point of the text unless the *effect* of the text, whether intended or not – allowing the text to rouze one's faculties to act – stirs and engages. That is what Blake understood so well and what he practised, even if at times we consider he may have got it wrong. In writing as he did Blake was amazingly prescient, as 200 years later biblical scholarship has begun to catch up with him, and to recognize that many biblical texts, whether prophetic oracles, or New Testament epistles, are texts that were written to have an effect, and understanding their rhetorical content is crucial to their meaning.

Like the biblical writers, Blake did not write in order either to offer an aesthetic experience or to be a source for history, but to challenge and to edify. Those who engage with Blake's works as tools of edification will be able to resonate with them and gain insights that may be missed by those who do not read in this way. Anthony Thiselton's words about the Bible apply *mutatis mutandis* to Blake's work (Thiselton 1992, p. 616).

Blake was a master at seeking to allow texts to have effects, and he appreciated why it is that the Bible, allusive and enigmatic as it might be in its different parts, was one of the paradigms for his own imaginative textual creation. Biblical allusions are dotted all over the Blake corpus. The biblical allusions form part of Blake's kaleidoscopic use of imagery, in which the various ingredients are used to produce ever-new arrangements of beauty, and visual and intellectual meaning.

Blake found in the images of the Bible a stimulus to the imagination and creativity in understanding the vagaries of human life. He didn't attempt to make the Bible internally consistent, or benevolent. He challenged its depiction of God as a remote monarch and lawgiver, and the use made of such imagery to justify authoritarianism. He saw the Bible being used as a means of keeping people in their places. So, subservience to what had been believed and done in the past ended up giving power to those who were responsible for knowing and transmitting these ideas, thereby snuffing out creativity and imagination. Blake had no truck with those who appealed to the past to maintain the status quo, or to a sacred text, rather than to what human beings, created in the divine image, may be saying now, or struggling to articulate, as they moved forward in their lives. He rejected the idea of the Bible as a divine rulebook, according to which priests and rulers could police people, but saw it as a collection of 'sentiments and examples' which engaged the imagination. His life work was dedicated to exposing the extent to which infatuation with those habits of thought separate and demonize, and prevent human flourishing. He had an amazing insight into contemporary economics, politics and culture, and was able to discern the effects of authoritarianism.

Blake's words, known as 'Jerusalem' (which are in fact a preface in some versions of his epic poem, *Milton*), set to music by Hubert Parry, have attracted traditional English and radical political activist alike. These stanzas epitomize not only an aspiration for a better world, but also one that comes, but through the struggle, the 'mental fight' as Blake calls it. For Blake the New Jerusalem is not something that needs to be a remote possibility, but something that may be built in 'England's green and pleasant land'. There is no disjunction between human activity and divine activity, nothing here about 'leaving it all to God', because God indwells men and women who are capable through the imaginative and creative work of the artist to shed light on the present. Building the New Jerusalem is a task that is open to all. At the end of his poem Blake quotes some words from the Bible: 'Would to God that all the LORD's people were prophets,' (Numbers 11.29). The primacy of 'the Poetic Genius which is every where call'd the Spirit of Prophecy' is fundamental to all religion (*All Religions Are One* 5; E1). What is more, as he put it in some candid marginal notes he made in a book by the Bishop of Llandaff on Tom Paine's views on the Bible, prophecy is not some kind of specialist task from which some are exempt. 'Every honest man is a Prophet he utters his opinion both of private & public matters' (Annotations to Watson's 'Apology', 14; E617).

Prophecy for Blake was telling the truth as best one can about what one sees, fortified by an 'honest persuasion'. Blake wanted to stir people from their intellectual slumbers, to see that they were captivated in the grip of a culture that kept them thinking in ways that served the interests of the powerful.

Blake was a pioneer of Dietrich Bonhoeffer's 'religionless Christianity' (Bonhoeffer 1981). The Church – and indeed religion – is part of the problem not the solution, because it has become an end in itself. Blake does not have too much to say about Paul, but what he does say is critical, despite the fact that elements of Pauline theology are crucial to his understanding of the way in which the divine life is lived in and among humans. There are two references wherc he makes Paul the founder of the Church, a tradition that has its story running through history, including Constantine and the Holy Roman Empire down to the Magisterial Reformation and its effects on English religion down to his own day (e.g. *Milton* 24:32, E120).

In the Bible Blake found his basic conviction that the Gospel was the Forgiveness of Sins ('The Gospel is Forgiveness of Sins & has No Moral Precepts', Blake's annotation to Richard Watson's 'Apology', E619). He rebelled against its politics and its elevation of holiness and the sense of separation and negation. The forgiveness of sins required learning about 'Contraries' and understanding not rejection and a sense of moral superiority but engagement with the Other. His statement 'Without Contraries is no progression' (*Marriage of Heaven and* Hell 3, E34) epitomizes his rejection of dualistic ways of thinking and the espousal in oneself and so in others of the understanding of difference. 'Inside' and 'outside', the sacred and the profane, and the Body of Christ as an exclusive entity, are all concepts contrary to Blake's vision of universal brotherhood based on the recognition of the divine within every human. For Blake it is not a matter of opting into some special ark of salvation but recognizing that one is already in. He saw more clearly than anyone that the Church's life too readily sets up false dichotomies between sacred and profane whose very preservation and institutionalization becomes an end in itself.

For Blake that which has been handed down must always take second place to the Poetic Genius and the Spirit of Prophecy latent in every one. Blake recognizes the past but gives himself the imaginative space to engage with it critically and insightfully. That can stir the embers of the past and fan into flame new insight and wisdom as a result. Blake exemplifies for me the necessary task of 'clearing an imaginative space' with regard to authoritative texts and traditions (Bloom 1997, p. 5), recognizing their shortcomings as well as being empowered by the inspiration they offered. In so doing, as Ronald Paulson has so concisely and illuminatingly put it, Blake shows himself to be 'a great illustrator of the repressed text who brings out its latent meaning which has been covered over by pious and tendentious commentators … [he] exposes the errors of the actual verbal and visual text of the Bible while preserving their truths' (Paulson 1982, p. 118).

Blake sought to find a way of confining imaginative energy into a form that might communicate with those who read and view his works. Art, life and prophecy overlap, for all are creations to deal with the particular, determined by the limits of context and the medium of one's activities. His images and texts were about 'wresting tradition away from a conformism that is about to overpower it' (Benjamin 'Theses' VI, 1992, p. 247, also quoted in Ferber 1985, p. 201). That included awareness of the extent to which the human ego can lead to counter-productive endeavours that do not lead to 'Human Brotherhood' (*Jerusalem* 96.16, 21, 28, E255–6). In 1 Corinthians 13 Paul writes about the temporary nature of prophecy and the permanent need for charity: 'Charity never faileth: but whether there be prophecies, they shall fail' (13.8). Prophecy is a phenomenon of the present age which can assist us as 'we see through a glass, darkly' until such time as we see 'face to face'; meanwhile we 'know in part' (1 Cor. 13.12, KJV). No one understood better that the 'Poetic Genius, the Spirit of Prophecy' had to be informed by an altruistic element. Blake carved out an imaginative space with regard to authoritative texts and traditions whether it is the literary legacy of John Milton or the Bible, recognizing their shortcomings as well as being inspired by what they offered him. The peculiar mixture of imaginative existential engagement of the Bible, along with criticism of its shortcomings, articulates and encapsulates a brilliant paradigm.

Blake's work, particularly his writing about and visual exegesis of the Bible, has given me a way of learning to be critical about myself and also about the shortcomings of the Bible, as well as finding in the Bible a word of life. The 'contrapuntal/dialectical engagement with life' and with the biblical writings, to which we refer below, not only helps me understand Blake but also helps me see an analogy with the way I engage with texts from at least 2,000 years ago and for all their shortcomings find in them hope and comfort as well as critical insight.

Reflections

Engaging with Ruskin (for Zoë) and Blake (for Christopher) has provided us with analogies for the critical understanding of the Bible and life in our own time. The use of a historical figure in this way offers a kind of contrapuntal/dialectical engagement with life and with the writings that inform us. Each person has a unique critical space that will do the job for them, so we are not wanting to say that everyone must use historical figures like Ruskin and Blake. What we see in our own work is the way that a journey with others has been an important part of what criticism – of the Bible and of life – is about.

Although their contexts, life histories and personalities were utterly different, there are concerns and attitudes that overlap between Blake and Ruskin in their engagement with the Bible. They are both concerned that the Bible should not be used to oppress either the minds or the bodies of their fellow human beings. Authoritarian imposition, the 'binding with briars my heart and desires', and the suppression of imagination and critical engagement were anathema to both. Likewise the use of the Bible to justify political and economic oppression, to destroy human bodies and spirits, they both rejected, finding instead in the images, the injunctions and the stories of the Bible possibilities for communal human flourishing. Notwithstanding this, neither of them has any problem with taking issues with elements in the

Bible that they feel are inimical to human flourishing. For both, the Church was part of the problem, and Christian exclusivity a mean-minded dead-end road to nowhere. For both prophecy was about telling the truth as one sees it.

Seeing well and truly, while being a crucial critical activity for both Blake and Ruskin, was understood and practised rather differently by each of them. Ruskin had the 'eye of a bird' (Drury 2000) – picking out detailed particulars, of leaves and blades of grass, of rock formations and gothic architecture, of the gold lettering in a medieval Bible manuscript and the minutiae of translation, and of the poverty and pain of those on the underside of the industrial revolution. His epistemology is in this way strongly empiricist, and his understanding informed by the straightforward details of all he saw physically. Nevertheless, for Ruskin 'heart-sight' was as important as eyesight; and the penetrative imagination more important than the recording of visually perceived information:

> You do not see *with* the lens of the eye. You see *through* that, and by means of that, but you see with the soul of the eye ... Sight is an absolutely spiritual phenomenon ... (Cook and Wedderburn 1903–12, 22.194–95)

Blake, too, picks out detailed particulars as in 'Holy Thursday' (*Songs of Innocence*) and 'London' (*Songs of Experience*). But throughout for Blake images and texts are the launching pad for flights of imaginative engagement:

> If the Spectator could Enter into these Images in his Imagination, approaching them on the Fiery Chariot of his Contemplative Thought if he could enter into Noah's Rainbow or into his Bosom, or could make a Friend & Companion of one of these Images of wonder which always intreats him to leave mortal things as he must know then would he arise from his Grave then would he meet the Lord in the Air [cf. 1 Thess. 4.17] & then he would be happy. ('A Vision of the Last Judgment', E560)

'For Ruskin, and for Blake,' writes Alan Davies, 'the issue of perception was never just an interesting subject for intellectual discussion. They were engaged in an urgent dialectic in which life, in its full, most vivid, inspired sense, was pitted against a kind of death through spiritual and imaginative poverty' (Davies 2006, p. 38). In the spirit of such imaginative engagement, and by way of laying bare how we have been enriched not only by our respective engagements with Blake and with Ruskin, but also by looking at analogies, comparisons and differences between them, we finish this chapter with a 'letter' written by Zoë to Blake and one written by Christopher to Ruskin.

Dear Mr Blake,

I am very taken with what you wrote about memory and inspiration. And if memory is experienced and seen as rote learning or just commentary I am entirely in agreement. But this seems to miss out something that is fundamental to my experience. Let me put it thus: holding within myself the memory of all I have learned about something – anything – and that memory may be of feelings, thoughts, conversations, things I have read – I experience a freedom in which inspiration often comes. Not just the capacity to conceive of something coherently, but new connections and illuminations, thoughts and understandings which take me beyond where I had got to. It's as if the relaxation that comes with familiarity with the territory is a fertile seedbed for inspiration. In this a certain sort of memory acts as a catalyst for inspiration.

On reflection this may be something to do with 'threshold concepts' and deep learning, so to do with liminality and with ownership and self-involvement. So if at the threshold I try to step further by learning by rote without true understanding and ownership I will never get anywhere. But if I have internalized and owned all that has got me to the threshold so I am at home with it, I have enough courage and imagination to grasp what takes me further.

This has implications for the bearing of tradition. It would seem that the very same thing – immersion in a tradition and the internalizing of it – within the memory – might be the cause of stultification (because all I then do is enjoy feeling at home but never ask 'does it have to be like this?') or it may be the ground on which I can stand to reach further and enter places that may fulfil my memory (my indwelling tradition), challenge it, contradict it, or relativize it.

There are problems with this. The first is that I have jumped by analogy, from a personal experience of writing and thinking, to a generalized theory of what might happen to other people and to communities. The second is that this account doesn't sufficiently acknowledge the feminist and other positions which find what is in the (cultural) memory far more problematic than my account here, in which it is essentially benign though contradictable in a nice liberal revisionist kind of way. The third problem, which is really part of the second, is that I haven't really taken account of how tenacious a 'tradition' is, how it is reinforced by ideological practices and cultural baggage, institutional vested interests, and the intellectual commitment of those who work by memory not by inspiration. So there is then no room for 'memory' to be the launching pad for inspiration and a much harder road must be trodden. One that rails against and rejects the process and products of memory as the murderer of inspiration.

In this discussion I see my perennial battle with colleagues to try and break them away from teaching the tradition in the guild-delineated subject areas. They say it gives a launching pad; I say it kills inspiration. So I am on your side Mr Blake but want to know how to give an account of the experience of memory with which I started this letter.

Yours truly,
Zoë Bennett

Dear Mr Ruskin

I have been fascinated and amazed by your annotations written on your copy of the medieval lectionary you had in your library. By our standards it seems a pretty iconoclastic act on your part, defacing an ancient manuscript. You wrote admiringly of William Blake's Job' engravings and compared them favourably with Rembrandt's work, though elsewhere you wrote of him being 'full of wild creeds and somewhat diseased in brain'. To digress: I share your delight in Turner's paintings yet have never been able to understand why you took against Whistler's Turner-esque painting. Turner and Blake both depicted the same passage in the Book of Revelation in their paintings entitled 'Death on a Pale Horse', inspired by Revelation 6.8. Both of these images capture something of the subject matter of Revelation. Blake's depicts the inexorable move of history towards its ending; Turner's painting picks up on the haze of battle and destruction hinted at in the words of Revelation and is altogether more mysterious and vague. For Blake distinct lines were important and how he depicted things reflect how he saw things in his visions (*Descriptive Catalogue* 64, 4a, E531, 550).

Both you and Blake revealed some of your most pungent criticisms about what you read in your marginal notes. Blake's were not directly on a biblical text, but both of you reveal your attitudes to what you read, whether it be the writings of contemporaries, or the Holy Bible or, in the case of Blake, a revered literary giant like Milton, in the form and content of your annotations. Neither of you approached the received text with reverence – far from it. What the text and its contemporary interpretation provoke from you tells me much about your attitude to contemporary religion and, more importantly, about the Bible as Holy Scripture. You are not afraid to write that you found some parts of the Greek text not just baffling but obfuscatory and unhelpful. So I appreciate how you annotated your lectionary in the way you did, not only revealing so much of yourself but also of your honesty in the way you understood the Bible.

Blake shared your irreverence towards sacred scripture. He problematized the notion of a single authoritative text by ensuring that his own artistic creations were variously illuminated and arranged in different, and to us often confusing, orders. And his treatment of the story of Job shows him taking issue with dominant biblical themes like divine monarchy and the theological dualism which is inherent in the idea of holiness. Much of his work especially of the 1790s is in fact a series of complex 'Notes on the Bishop's Book' as he termed his annotations to the Bishop of Llandaff's critique of Tom Paine. Blake was determined to unmask the way 'that Kings & Priests had copied on Earth' a supposedly divinely endorsed book (*Europe a Prophecy* 11.4, E64), and the way in which 'State tricksters' co-opted the Bible, thereby in their view imitating a God who endorses an authoritative book. The problem is that it is their hierarchical interpretation of it, which gives them their power and their ideological justification for their dominion over their fellow men and women.

You wrote about 'seeing' as the conduit of emotion and understanding. Such attentive seeing is an end in itself rather than a means to an end, or rather the necessary accumulation of disparate information which assists understanding and enables insight. Blake was a seer of a different kind, and the problem with some seers is that they offer an interpretation of what things *really* mean, unmasking the depths of the superficial. But for you depth is there in the comprehension of the totality of what is seen in all its variety and complexity. In contrast, Blake chastized those who relied on 'organs of sense', and instead invoked 'the Poetic or Prophetic Character' to stop 'the Philosophic & Experimental repeating "the same dull round over again"' (There is NO Natural Religion, V11, E3). I don't think he adequately appreciated your way of discerning the meaning of 'Minute Particulars'. The way the particulars were used by each of you differed. Whereas for Blake the particulars are taken up in the imagination and become the furniture of its new understanding, your focus on detail leads to better understanding of what is seen, as context and history, and how all enter to contribute to a different kind of imaginative reconstruction which may illuminate our understanding every bit as much as Blake's imaginative essays.

Finally, I want to return to a theme I touched on earlier in this letter. In his disastrous 1809 exhibition, Blake put his inner world on public display and received a devastating response in a review by Robert Hunt. That must have had its effect but, as far as we can discern, it was not catastrophic, either because this was something that Blake was used to dealing with or more likely that there was an inner confidence about his convictions based on his inner world. So, whatever the treatment when his pearls were thrown before the critical swine, he could retreat into that inner world, certain that it would offer convalescence. Rather presumptuously, I would like to suggest that the situation seems to have been rather different for you, as the inner world suddenly burst through into the reality of ordinary life in such an invasive way. As I ponder your later life, there seems to be extraordinary creativity in the fascination with St Ursula and the identification with your young friend Rose LaTouche, but I sense, perhaps wrongly, your later years were dominated by a state of mind that may pass for 'madness', which Blake lived with hour by hour.

Yours in gratitude and with profound appreciation,

Christopher Rowland

6
'Give me a place to stand'

Introduction

This chapter approaches the heart of how the Bible functions in our lives. Two words are crucial to understanding this: ideology and reflexivity. We take it as indisputably true that we, as all other human beings, are never in full possession of the truth and are never fully able to grasp what makes for human flourishing. It is our human predicament; but it is inescapable. Nothing, but nothing, is known by us without some distortion, and that includes all claims to knowledge by revelation. So it follows that we need to examine critically the taken-for-granted beliefs and practices of our society (their ideologies), and we need to examine ourselves in such a way as to give ourselves the best chance possible of seeing the partial and distorted (ideological) nature of our understanding. If the latter sounds a bit like trying to pull ourselves up by our own bootlaces, it is. However, there are some tools at our disposal, and the most important are the critique of ideology, and the practice of being self-reflexive.

'It doesn't have to be like this.' So the African-American feminist writer, bell hooks, describes why theory is an important tool to critique practice; and this same statement of questioning, of longing and of resistance lies at the heart of all ideological critique. Theory, in hooks' understanding, can be a 'place of healing' (hooks 1994, p. 61). Driven by the need to know why her father beat her, getting some critical distance on a hard-pressed African-American man struggling to bring up his family and survive in a racist society, she imagined a world in which it didn't have to be so. Theory is about finding some critical distance, about asking 'why' – which she says makes children the best theorists, always asking: 'Why?' It is about interrogating the underlying situation, above all about claiming the possibility of another world, of different ways of feeling and acting, of 'the practice of freedom'. In the words of Jesus in John's Gospel you 'will know the truth, and the truth will make you free' (8.32). To be a disciple of Jesus is to become like a little child (Matt. 18.1–5), and to see the world with fresh and questioning eyes and heart.

While it is undoubtedly true that the appreciative inhabiting of beliefs, practices, images and ideas is an element on the way to freedom and truth (and this book has in one sense been an account of many different forms of such appreciative inhabiting), it is also the case that a sense of inadequacy, of cognitive dissonance or of physical or emotional pain drives us to hope that 'it doesn't *have* to be like this'. Theoretical analysis, alternative imaginings, and contemporary or historical comparisons can all offer a way into a critical understanding.

Looking at examples from the Christian tradition, from main-stream and from more marginal sources, is crucial for gaining a critical theological perspective on one's context. Practical theology has long had to resort to theory, whether sociological, psychological or philosophical, to enable understanding and the clarity of expression that theory can offer. But 'theory' is not the only tool for the job. History can offer a critical perspective every bit as penetrating as social theory or philosophy. Historically it is philosophy that has, from the very first inroads of Platonism in the Alexandrian theology to the influence of Aristotle in the late Middle Ages and the Enlightenment philosophy of Locke and Kant, been the dominant dialogue partner of the Christian tradition. But, as many writing in a liberationist vein have argued, that does not have to be the only way, and social and political theory is equally important. So we consider how liberation and feminist theology and forgotten voices within the Christian tradition can help us to find new perspectives on life and the Bible.

The term 'hermeneutics of suspicion' refers to a way of interpreting texts, language, actions, institutions and beliefs which asks underlying questions of what is presupposed in them. So, in bell hooks' case, she questioned the need for frustration to find an outlet in violence, and behind that, she questioned the rightness of a society in which the hidden violence of racism was enshrined. Things do not have to be like this; there is another way. It has to be imagined, and it has to be worked for. Theory here is more about imagination – seeing, '*theoria*', 'vision' – than it is about abstraction or generalization.

What is questioned is the 'ideology', the taken-for-granted conditions of life and the legitimations of the status quo. That is an important component for critical reflexivity that is primarily informed by hope, and rejects the status quo as the ultimate good. Even if ideological criticism is not referred to explicitly in the Bible, the underlying characteristics of what we know as the criticism of ideology are found there. The challenge to ideology goes back deep into the memories of Jewish origins in the critique of Pharaoh and of idolatry which is embedded in the Bible, and surfaces with great power in the apocalyptic tradition represented by the Book of Revelation. The start of our work together was the exploration of the Book of Revelation as an ancient form of the critique of ideology as we considered in Chapter 1.

Contemporary public life is full of the ideological critique of religion from an 'outsider', or a partially 'outsider', position. From the writings of Richard Dawkins (2006) to the popular press, religion is seen as delusional and destructive. The Bible does not escape this critique; indeed the scriptures of faith communities are implicated in the fostering of fundamentalist positions and bigotry. Important though this issue is, it is not the subject matter of this book. Examples of engagement with this issue may be found in books by Elaine Graham and Alister McGrath and Joanna Collicutt McGrath (Graham 2013; McGrath and Collicutt McGrath 2007).

In this chapter we focus attention on other forms of ideology critique in relation to the Bible: insider critique – ideological critique found within the Bible of the religion also contained within the Bible, outward focused critique of society using the Bible, and self-critique – which we explore through a consideration of reflexivity and, as a challenging conclusion, the quest for critical self-reflexiveness in the application of *The Spiritual Exercises of Ignatius Loyola* (1491–1556).

What is ideology?

'Ideology' is one of those words that is used in a variety of different ways (Larrain 1992; Eagleton 2007). So, even theology can be deemed ideological in the way in which a ruling elite upholds ideas that support the interests of the institution they serve and the power they exercise in it. That is the way the term was taken up and used within the Marxist tradition, outlined in Karl Marx's *The German Ideology* (Marx and Engels 1998), to indicate the way in which ideas are intimately related to the struggle for power and hegemony and particularly the ways in which ruling elites promote their values by recourse to 'ideologies' that are deemed to be natural or normal but in fact serve their own interests. Thereby the majority of the people, by subscribing unwittingly to such ideas in their culture and everyday lives, are unaware that they are supporting the interests of their rulers and other powerful groups. In *The German Ideology* Marx and Engels start from 'real human beings', who must produce their means of subsistence in order to satisfy their material needs. So, material life conditions social life. The political and legal institutions of society are explained by the nature of the economic structure. The nature of a society's ideology, its religious, artistic, moral and philosophical belief, is determined by its economic structure and the wielders of economic power.

Ernst Bloch and Walter Benjamin: the messianic critique of ideology

Marxist philosophers such as Ernst Bloch (Bloch 1986, 2009) have noted the internal ideological critique in early Christian discourse. For example, he contrasts Jesus, the Son of Man coming on the clouds of heaven to establish justice for the poor, with the Lord Christ, enthroned in heaven in a glorious state similar to the imperial oppressors of the poor. He shows how the former expectation has moved to the margins of the Christian tradition, ostracized by the exponents of the dominant ideology. Gradually, this Son of Man belief has been displaced by the divine Kyrios, Lord, a title that, as he puts it, 'admirably suited the purposes of those who would reduce the Christian community to a sort of military service of their cultic hero' (2009, p. 36). So language about Jesus the Kyrios took the place of the apocalyptic maverick who died on a Roman gallows.

According to Bloch the Second Coming reveals the real point of the Ascension to be the transformation of heaven prior to the descent of the New Jerusalem from heaven to earth to be the city of humanity. Bloch's utopian vision, illuminating forgotten paths and sensitive to the growth of ideology, goes alongside his repeated emphasis on the present need to live *as if* the new age were here. Bloch considers that the utopian is at the heart of human experience and is already at hand in an anticipatory and fragmentary way. These fragments are themselves an encouragement to human action in the present. Utopia is not fully possible within the limitations of the present order of things, but he disputes the view that utopianism is merely a retreat into a fantasy world, for the vision of a better world is the other side of the coin of the unmasking of political and economic power. It requires discovering the cracks offered on the cliff-face of history to survive and inhabit in the face of the seemingly impregnable dominant power and its ideology.

Also, from the Marxist tradition, in his striking messianic tract written at the very end of his life as he faced persecution and death, Walter Benjamin wrote that

> in every era the attempt must be made anew to wrest tradition away from conformism that is about to overpower it. The Messiah comes not only as the redeemer, he comes as the subduer of Antichrist. Only that historian will have the gift of fanning the spark of hope in the past who is firmly convinced that *even the dead* will not be safe from the enemy if he wins. And this enemy has not ceased to be victorious (Benjamin, *Thesis* VI, 1992, p. 247).

Apocalyptic 'unmasking' helps show that cultural monuments, venerable texts, artifacts and institutions – celebrated by official, establishment history – cannot be understood outside the context of their origins, a context of oppression and exploitation: 'there is no document of civilization which is not at the same time a document of barbarism. And just as such a document is not free of barbarism, barbarism taints also the manner in which it was transmitted from one owner to another' (Benjamin, *Thesis* VI, p. 248). The unmasking enabled by apocalypse is available in 'the present as the "time of the now" which is shot through with chips of Messianic time' (Benjamin, *Thesis* A, p. 255).

Varieties of ideological critique

There are several possible forms that the 'critique of ideology' might take in relation to biblical texts:

- Ideological critique found within the Bible of the religion and/or scriptures also contained within the Bible – an 'insider' critique.
- Ideological critique of particular interpretations and/or

uses of the Bible.

- Ideological critique of contemporary society and its beliefs and practices *by* the Bible.
- Ideological critique of our own (individual and communal) beliefs and practices.

Insider critique

There are many examples of challenge to ideology in the Bible, not least when the oppressed Hebrew slaves on the verge of a degree of freedom for themselves look back to the ideology of Egypt and its culture in those memorable words from Exodus 16.3: 'If only we had died by the hand of the LORD in the land of Egypt, when we sat by the fleshpots and ate our fill of bread; for you have brought us out into this wilderness to kill this whole assembly with hunger.' In the Hebrew Bible apologists for priests and kings and other elites may have their say but the pages of this remarkable collection, as two centuries of biblical scholarship has shown, evince different kinds of power struggles between priest and prophet, between true and false prophet, between one holy place, Jerusalem in particular, and the rest, and between those who supported the institution of kingship and those who did not. To describe this as an ideological struggle is entirely appropriate.

So, the critique of ideology is not an alien imposition upon the Bible and Christian discourse. The prophetic critique of the 'sacred canopy' of religion (Berger 1967), *from within the religion itself*, is a strong feature of both the New Testament and the Hebrew Bible, the totality of Christian 'scripture'. Just as the prophets critiqued the self-serving powerful elite, and Jesus placed the poor, the lowly and the outcast at the centre of God's kingdom, so later Christian communities are called by this 'golden thread' of texts within texts to question and to resist the unjust structures of society and religion in their own day. So, argues Radford Ruether, Jesus may not, could not, have been a 'feminist', but the feminist critique of Christianity in our day 'correlates' with Jesus' critique of his own religion in his own time. This is an *internal* critique of religion. Thus liberationist biblical hermeneutics has been crucial in promoting ideological criticism (Segundo 1976; Rowland and Corner 1990).

Ideological critique of contemporary society and its beliefs and practices by the Bible

While in Christian radicalism and in feminist theology we find the Bible critiqued insofar as it has obscured, legitimated, even engendered and encouraged, oppression, we also find the Bible creatively and imaginatively used to critique the status quo and as a powerful tool in the cause of human flourishing. The existing conditions of life, and legitimating ideologies, are critiqued by the Bible; that is the Bible itself may offer a critique of current practices, understandings and beliefs in both religious and secular spheres.

Anthony Thiselton distinguishes between a socio-pragmatic approach and a socio-critical approach in hermeneutics. In the first the social conditions are uncritically accepted and there is no critique of present practice. This can happen in lazy or uncritical forms of practical theology, where experience and practice are the starting point of theological reflection but are taken for granted and are never themselves exposed to critique. In the second, the socio-critical approach, the Bible itself becomes a powerful tool to critique present conditions (1992, Chapter XII). Such a socio-critical approach is seen in Chapter 5, where John Ruskin and William Blake are seen to offer a critique of their contemporary society inextricably linked with their understanding of the Bible.

Earlier we wrote that 'unmasking' and 'the horizon of hope' merge in the New Testament Apocalypse, which is why it has been such an important factor in discerning how and why we negotiate the ongoing creation of a critical space. 'Unmasking' is a word we have used on several occasions to describe the process of the exercise of criticism and discernment. The theology of hope is compellingly described by Moltmann as a thorn in the side of the present (Moltmann 2002, p. 21 and above p. 104). John of Patmos's apocalyptic visions drew on an emerging prophetic critique of empire and are a loud protest against a dominant ideology. This book of prophecy is full of counter-cultural items: its language and symbolism; its emphasis on witness and prophecy and the lack of any conventional 'churchiness' (unlike the Pauline letters), comfort for the prophetic faithful only. The visions of Revelation do not provide the currency of our everyday exchange of ideas and patterns of existence. Like the most pungent political cartoon, John's imagery challenges and may probe the defences of human complacency. In antiquity, visions and dreams proved to be a potent force for offering an alternative perspective.

Dietrich Bonhoeffer seems to have glimpsed something of the

interpretative potential of the Book of Revelation in its ability to challenge the 'Laodicean' culture (cf. Rev. 3.15–20) by unmasking the character of Christian compromise and the Beast of nationalism and oppression when he exhorted fellow church men and women to be 'a community which hears the Apocalypse ... to testify to its alien nature and to resist the false principle of innerworldliness' and so to be at the service of 'those who suffer violence and injustice'. In his view 'the Church takes to itself all the sufferers, (all) the forsaken of every party and status', 'Open your mouth for the dumb' (Prov. 31.8; Bonhoeffer 1965, pp. 324–5). In the Germany of the 1930s the Book of Revelation, so often suspected in the Lutheran tradition, offered a resource for theology which enabled another perspective on the terrible events through which Bonhoeffer and his contemporaries were living. It is not surprising that the Book of Revelation, and the apocalyptic tradition generally, has often been linked to projects of social change. Alongside more reactionary uses, apocalyptic symbolism can serve to enable the oppressed to find and maintain a critical distance from an unjust world – bringing hope and holding out the prospect of a reign of justice.

Gerrard Winstanley (c. 1625–76): A seventeenth-century ideological unmasking

Gerrard Winstanley was a seventeenth-century practitioner of ideological criticism, and in many ways took on the baton of his apocalyptic predecessors. Winstanley shot to prominence in 1649 and then almost completely disappeared from the annals of history for the rest of his life (he died in 1676). He grasped the moment of the execution of King Charles I to seize what he (and many others) thought was an opportunity to establish a different kind of society, and he interpreted that moment in the light of the Bible as a word for his time. Winstanley engaged dynamically with the imagery of the Book of Daniel and the Book of Revelation—particularly the references to the beasts arising from the sea—as a means to comprehending the oppressive political powers that kept the common people in thrall. Perhaps his most daring interpretation was of Genesis 2–3, the story of 'the Fall'. For Winstanley, the Fall meant that humans had turned towards a life of 'covetousness' and the maintenance of self-centredness, institutionalized in private property and the social fabric that maintained inequality, and justified by theology, when the earth should have been originally a 'common treasury' for all to share. Winstanley's theological hope was that this situation may be overcome through 'consciousness raising', which might thereby lead to a restoration of humankind to a very different vision of the world grounded in justice and equality.

In his version of ideological criticism, a reading of the Bible is offered in which the social and political combine with the exegetical to enable an engagement with the Bible and to read it 'relative to life', as the liberation exegete Carlos Mesters puts it (Mesters 1989, 1993). In his unmasking of the nature of contemporary power relations Winstanley relates the beasts of Daniel 7 to the oppressive behaviour of the wielders of political and economic power of his day: royal power, which by force makes a way for the economically powerful to rule over others; the power of the legal system, which maintains power and privilege in the hands of the few; what Winstanley calls 'the thieving Art of buying and selling, the Earth with the fruits one to another'; and finally the power of religion to give a religious or (in something like Marx's sense) an ideological gloss to the privileges of the few ('Fire in the Bush', Corns, Hughes and Loewenstein 2009, ii.190–6). According to Winstanley the Creation will never be at peace until these four beasts are overthrown, and only then will there be the coming of Christ's kingdom.

Winstanley's writings offer us an example of someone who availed himself of apocalyptic imagery, in his case from the Book of Daniel, in order to understand the reality of the situation in which he lived and the struggles in which he and his colleagues found themselves involved in the wake of the execution of Charles 1 and the political opportunities that seemed to offer.

Ideological critique of our own (individual and communal) beliefs and practices: learning to be self-reflexive

The philosopher Hegel (1770–1831) discusses the detachment that is typical of historical study of the Bible, which, whatever its other virtues, can miss the political character of its own discourse and the extent to which its exponents are themselves implicated in maintaining the citadels of power in their own day or unaware of the extent to which there may have been similar struggles going on within and behind the biblical text:

> It is to be noted that there is a type of theology that wants to adopt *only a historical attitude* towards religion; it even has an abundance of cognition, though only of a historical kind. This cognition is no concern of ours, for if the cognition of religion were merely historical, we would have to compare

> such theologians with counting-house clerks, who keep the ledgers and accounts of other people's wealth, a wealth that passes through their hands without their retaining any of it, clerks who act only for others without acquiring any assets of their own. They do of course receive a salary, but their merit lies only in keeping records of the assets of other people. In philosophy and religion, however, the essential thing is that one's own spirit itself should recognize a possession and content, deem itself worthy of cognition, and not keep itself humbly outside. (Hegel 1984, p. 128)

Detachment, according to Hegel, is an impoverished form of knowledge, for it ignores our part in maintaining certain ideas and values. For Hegel true knowledge and the knower are inseparable, as also the knower is inseparable from that which is known, be it nature, the human community, or God. As the title of one of the most distinguished modern critical theorists writing in the Marxist tradition Jürgen Habermas suggests, knowledge and human interest are inextricably interwoven (Habermas 1987). That applies as much to their modern interpreters as to the biblical authors themselves.

Self-knowledge is as vital as awareness of one's social context. There is a typical syndrome of academic study, in which knowledge about what is professed is what counts rather than experience in one's personal life, so that the 'professional' is distinguished from the 'personal'. We want to question that distinction, particularly in the intellectual quest for a critical engagement with the Bible. Failure to include the personal, the contextual and the visionary in engagement with the Bible not only makes us individually 'counting house clerks' but is in danger of being, in Ernst Käsemann's striking words, quoted earlier, consumers of 'religious canned goods' (Käsemann 2010, p. 138–9).

If objectivity is neither desirable nor even attainable, it is essential that the subjectivity we embrace is a *critical subjectivity*. Critique demands reflection. In this book we have begun the work of reflection through the telling of stories. These have been stories in which we had a part, but they have not been stories of ourselves as isolated individuals, but as people who belong in relationship to others, a part of communities in which we are not totally absorbed but of which we are not totally independent. To tell a story is to begin to make meaning of the events and contexts in that story. The story that Zoë and her husband told a few days after Thomas died was already putting significant meanings onto that story, struggling with how and where God was in it. Her sermon over 30 years later was still struggling with those questions. In both cases that struggle had deep roots in experience (illness, pain, death and hope), in the beliefs and practices of the communities of which she was a part at the time (evangelical youth work, preaching in a Cambridge College Chapel) and deep roots in the Bible (the Psalms, John's Gospel). The 'story' of her Christian belief in relation to Thomas's death has no single pinned-down meaning. Each time it is retold she constructs new meaning in the light of fresh understandings, beliefs, and experiences, and it is never finished. Telling it again here requires a further step – seeking to understand the process of the constructions of meaning, seeking a certain critical distance not only on the events but on her various tellings of the story. This process demands both a critical perspective on the ideologies at work, and a self-reflexive stance towards her own history and meaning-construction.

To see your own reflection is not necessarily to know the full 'truth' about yourself; nor is seeking to see your own reflection always a safe practice, as the story of Narcissus demonstrates, luminously portrayed in Caravaggio's painting of that name. The reflection is always in some way blurred or distorted, and the act of leaning closer to the pool is fraught with the danger of drowning, in which we merge with our reflection and see nothing. The self who sees and the self who is seen can never be identical.

Furthermore, the image of looking into a pool of water, or a bedroom mirror, is too simple to denote the practice of self-reflexivity. Anyone who has visited Chicago and seen Anish Kapoor's 'Cloud Gate', popularly known as 'the Bean', will have seen a vastly more complex form of 'self-reflection'. In this massive sculpture with a highly reflective surface of seamless stainless steel plates, curved and shaped like a bean, your reflection is distorted by the curves and given a context within the also-distorted reflections of the crowd, the clouds and the skyscrapers of downtown Chicago. As you move and look from another angle your own reflection changes. People take pictures of themselves taking pictures of themselves, taking pictures of themselves. The process of self-reflexivity is infinitely regressive. The more clarity the more mystery, leading to more clarity and thence to more mystery. This is the heart of the ongoing task of self-reflexivity. To do it comprehensively, we need to engage in a critique of our own beliefs and practices which takes seriously our own reflection on our individual pathology and context, both social and individual. In this the critique of ideology can assist us in our understanding of our social context. In the task of seeing and understanding our own reflection psychotherapy and the Ignatian tradition can assist us.

The analogy with psychotherapy

Finding analogies with psychotherapy can help us in our reflexivity. This need not be a narcissistic endeavour concerned only with our own pathology, but a way of understanding the dynamic of what is going on in all sorts of human interactions (Lomas 1981; 1987). An important resource for anyone seeking to learn from both social and psychological theory is the work of Jürgen Habermas. He has illuminated the connections between the therapeutic relationship and textual hermeneutics. In *Knowledge and Human Interests* (1987; Rowland 1996) Habermas suggests a connection between the psychological condition and the nature of texts. In both cases what he calls 'muted and distorted texts' need interpretation to show how their authors may be deceiving themselves' (1987, p. 252; Jameson 2002). In other words there is a parallel between the situation that confronts the psychotherapist and the exegete. For the former there are presenting symptoms and an increasingly obvious manifestation of those symptoms in the way in which the relationship between client and professional works itself out. For the latter, the personal and social effects of authoritative texts and the distortions and conflicts that informed those texts are the very stuff of the task of biblical exegesis.

Therapy enables the coming to consciousness of repressed thoughts and feelings and thereby allows some disentangling of past and present. So a distance can be established from the original experiences, and hidden assumptions and fears may be examined. As a result resistance can be established to the hegemony of the past so that the unconscious feelings no longer debilitate or paralyse the client. Such a process of distancing is necessary in interpretation of any kind, so that assumptions and habitual or unthought-through credence to a text or tradition may be examined and attention given to the reasons why there may be resistance to a text or too ready acceptance of its contents on the part of the reader.

In the therapeutic relationship there will be two dimensions: historical and contemporary. The former will involve the discovery of the details of the client's story which will enable some sense to be made of how an individual got to the present state of affairs and how it relates to present attitudes and feelings. But of equal importance, particularly where the experience of transference is concerned, and more often neglected, is the dynamics of the present interaction between therapist and client. Ways of relating with the therapist enable the hidden past to become apparent in the present. In biblical interpretation the historical approach has been refined and tested over the years and has been the foundation of critical study of the Bible. There has been much more unease about what counts as a distorted reading and finding appropriate criteria to discern the extent to which prejudice conditions, and even distorts, reading. But it is precisely here that a self-aware contextual theology in all its various forms has stimulated discussion and emphasized the need for attention to *where* reading is done and the effect of text on interpreter and vice versa. We need to ask ourselves: why do we allow ourselves to be carried along by a text or a particular way of reading; does our resistance to a text, biblical and otherwise, say more about ourselves than it does about the text; and is it necessary to resist co-opting the text to our agenda, to allow the problem posed by the space that opens up between ourselves and the text to be more fully understood? No critically reflective reader, practitioner or researcher is going to be free from the kind of intellectual engagement a necessarily self-involved reading and the reflection on it throw up.

Self-criticism and The Spiritual Exercises of Ignatius Loyola

In outlining the nature of criticism we have turned principally to modern writers like Marx and Freud, and the critical traditions they set in train. But self-reflexivity has always been a crucial part of the Christian tradition, probably going back to the Pauline letters in the New Testament, as was suggested in Chapter 2. As such it complements the psychotherapeutic tradition just discussed and the political critique that itself has a long history in the prophetic and apocalyptic texts of the Bible, which has been picked up by writers down the centuries. One well-established example of self-examination are *The Spiritual Exercises of Ignatius Loyola*. The Exercises have proved down the centuries to be a profound learning experience, expanding the horizons of many in their quest to be critically reflexive. As Joseph Munitiz puts it, *The Spiritual Exercises of Ignatius Loyola* (1491–1556):

> originated in the form of prayer notes, outlines of sequences of thoughts that had helped Ignatius as he reflected in silence before God. They take on meaning only in that sort of context

> ... When removed from their context they become as pointless as swimming instructions given to somebody who has no access to water. (2004, p. x)

Elsewhere, he writes of the text enabling someone to

> face God with honesty. In some ways this is no more mysterious than walking or running, but, just as most people would agree that reading a book is not the most helpful way to learn to walk or run, so any one who has actually experienced praying to God for light about the honesty of one's life will acknowledge that books are no great help. (Munitiz and Endean, pp. x, 281)

The Exercises offer a process of rigorous self-reflection rooted in assessment of the ways in which habits of life can so easily mask self-centredness set in the context of service of God and neighbour. It can be an experience of being searched out and known, as the Psalmist puts it (Ps. 139.1). That may well extend to parts of oneself jealously cherished as being most akin to the spirit of Christ but which may all too easily be subtly co-opted into a regime of fear, defensiveness, self-repute and self-aggrandizement, thereby undermining a true sense of self and vocation. Undertaking the Exercises is not so much about overcoming the patterns of a lifetime, but seeing more clearly the ways in which preoccupation with self is impoverishing to one's deepest sense of oneself and the way one relates to others. The Exercises are a mixture of recommendations for meditative reflection as well as a guide to imaginative engagement with the gospel narratives, a matter considered in the next chapter, whose impact depends on the experience of engaging with them rather than describing their contents (as pointed out in the quotation below). The experience of the Exercises can offer what Nietzsche called the 'revaluation of all values'.

The words 'when removed from their context [the Exercises] become as pointless as swimming instructions given to somebody who has no access to water' exactly characterize their character. The words are meant to be used, reflected and acted upon, not studied. In this respect, as indicated by some words written 20 years ago by Christopher, both liberation theology and the Ignatian Spiritual Exercises enable self-reflexivity:

> Liberation theology is a way, a discipline, an exercise which has to be lived rather than acquired as a body of information. It has its parallels in the classic texts of Western Christian spiritualty. *The Spiritual Exercises of Ignatius of Loyola*, the founder of the Jesuits, for example, seems at first sight to be a ragbag of Christian platitudes. To read them, without putting the advice into practice for oneself, however, fails to do justice to the fact that it is only when one actually *uses* them that the significance and function of the Exercises becomes apparent. What one is offered in them is a means of intellectual and ethical re-orientation. Similarly engagement with the texts of liberation theology offers an understanding of God from within a commitment to the poor and marginalized and a means of thinking afresh about reality or the ways we articulate it to one another. Therein lies their peculiar power. (Rowland 2007, p. 4)

Neither liberation theology nor the Spiritual Exercises are just about theological information, for both involve learning to live by means of the renewed perspectives they offer. They are ways of engaging in the 'revaluation of all values' which is that to which the constant process of critical reflexivity beckons as any one touched by liberation theology or who has undertaken the Ignation Exercises knows (Rowland 1994; Hughes 2008).

Conclusion

In this chapter we have attempted to outline some of the ingredients that we think are important in our quest to find a critical space. When the Marxist tradition is viewed with such suspicion by Pope Francis, for example, who has contrasted unfavourably ideology with faith, it may seem strange for us to be linking Marxism and Christianity. But we consider that there is no escape from ideological critique as part of the Christian tradition and its effects. As we have sought to show, there are those within the Marxist tradition and those from the wider Christian tradition who have pointed to the ways in which apocalypticism and messianism are potentially components in helping one to understand the shortcomings of the present and our implicatedness in it. In different ways Ernst Bloch and Walter Benjamin exemplify this. Benjamin's knowledge of Jewish messianism and mysticism, thanks to his close friendship with the pioneer scholar of the Jewish mystical tradition, Gershom Scholem, is a case in point. These two 'outsiders' anticipate what we have done and send us back with fresh eyes to the Christian tradition to find examples of the critique of ideology such as we find in the remarkable writings of the seventeenth-century writer Gerrard Winstanley. He was already part of long tradition of immersion in apocalypticism and its contribution to political critique. Hegel pointed us to the importance of self-awareness to deepen our criticism and that has been underlined by the importance attached to personal self-reflexivity, recognized in certain strands of Marxism as well as within the Ignatian tradition of Christian spirituality. The different sites of ideology – social, textual and personal – cannot be separated from each other and need to be kept in a mutually informative dialectical relationship in the reflective life.

7
An Emerging Map

Introduction

In these final chapters we present two critical processes. In Chapter 7 we revisit the key themes and methods of interpretation which have emerged in the course of this work, and offer a picture of how these elements might belong in a coherent whole. In Chapter 8 we reflect on the differences in the ways we relate to and interpret the Bible. There is a tension between these two processes; the differences offer a fault-line that resists any totalizing 'method' or 'model' of interpretation.

Our starting point is the desire to understand what it means to live a human life in such a way that we flourish. That 'we' is ecumenical, related to the whole inhabited world, the *oikoumene*, indicating our belief that the true flourishing of a human being is never in isolation from friends and neighbours, nor from the global community of human beings in their social and environmental context. To live and flourish as a human being is to be reflective, to live a reflective and examined life; as Socrates had it: 'for a human being the unexamined life is not worth living'.

As Christians we are reflective against a particular horizon of hope. That hope has its heart in the story of Jesus. It is displayed in the eschatological and apocalyptic texts of the Bible which summon us to a new way of seeing and understanding, of living and of desiring, to a new way of conceiving and imagining. The hope that frames our faith also questions our lives – 'it doesn't have to be like this' – and in so doing joins forces with the particularities of human existence, the 'grit in the shoe of life', to furnish the impetus and the material for a reflective life.

To reflect is to examine critically. To reflect we therefore need to find a critical space. Such a 'space' cannot, by the nature of human life, be detached either from the particularities of life or from the community or person reflecting. It can only be done in the midst of life, and is hard-won. Much of our book has addressed that battle – demonstrating in practice the negotiation of inevitably imperfect critical and imaginative spaces in the flow of life, and examining some of the strategies we have used in those negotiations.

The Bible is an indispensable tool in Christian critical imagination. Its stories, visions and prophecies, statements of faith and cries of despair, offer a rich invitation and challenge to reflect on human life. This book has not primarily been about criticism of the Bible, though it has elements of that; nor has it been primarily about the critique offered by the Bible to human life, personal and communal, though it has certainly included that. What we have wanted to persuade you, the reader, is that the Bible can enable individuals and communities to live reflective lives. Struggling to be critical human beings in the everyday world, not accepting injustice nor being content with banality, finding ways to question our own taken-for-granted perceptions and entrenched practices, we find in the Bible a lens through which to see our world more clearly, a vision of the opened heavens to inflame our 'arrows of desire', and a *vade mecum*, a 'go with me', a practical ready-reference that we carry about with us in our pockets or in our hearts, not to tell us what to do, but to challenge us that 'it doesn't have to be like this', and to offer us stories for our imaginative engagement and encouragement, stories of other human beings struggling imperfectly to live lives faithful to their fellow human beings and faithful to God.

There is another indispensable tool for reflective life, and that is the willingness to 'put ourselves on the page'. This also can never be a perfect process, not least because the self we know is never identical to the self who knows. As the Johari Window (Luft and Ingham 1955) indicates, two quadrants of our lives are unknown to us. But two quadrants *are* known, and the process of critical self-reflexivity begins, like Socratic questioning, to draw out what is in the hidden quadrants.

Such 'subjectivity' is often characterized as a lack of a critical perspective or academic credibility. So-called 'objectivity' is held up as the opposite of subjectivity, as the way to true knowledge, and, especially pertinent to the subject of this book, as the Holy Grail of biblical exegesis by which all else is judged. It is this category mistake, and all that flows from it, which lies at the heart of our discontent with the methodology of much of the last 200 years of academic biblical scholarship. That being critical involves not being subjective is a half-truth at best. Much of what we have written about is the necessity of the quest for a critical space that will give us a different perspective on ourselves, on our world and what we read. To that extent it is also a quest that resembles the quest for objectivity. We do not think that resort to detached historical reconstruction, which ignores ourselves as 'self-involved readers', is going to lead us to that

Holy Grail. It is impossible to split the knower and the known object cleanly or completely. At one level this means that examination of our own perspectives and prejudices helps clarify omissions or distortions in what we think we know. At a deeper level, such examination yields positive gains in understanding. An autobiographical narrative methodology is at one with the heart of biblical faith. In the words of Nicholas Lash, who was a creative and formative influence on both of us, and to whose work much of our thinking owes a great debt:

> the paradigm or 'focal' forms of Jewish and Christian religious discourse are not simply narrative but are, more specifically, autobiographical. They are autobiographical both in the sense that they are 'self-involving' (although this will be shown in their performance, and will not necessarily appear in their grammatical form) and in the sense that, as self-involving, they 'locate' the speaker (or the group of which he is a spokesman) in a particular cultural, historical tradition: 'My father was a wandering Aramean.' [Deut. 26.5] Whether the 'audience' addressed is God (in acts of supplication and worship) or other people (in acts of witness), the Christian is the teller of a tale, the narrator of a story that he tells as *his* story, as a story in which he acknowledges himself to be a participant. (Lash, 1986, pp. 101–2)

But, as Lash also points out, our stories, especially our autobiographical stories, need to be subjected to critique:

> on the one hand, the storyteller comes first inasmuch as Christian religious discourse, as a constitutive element in the practice of Christianity, is paradigmatically narrative (and, more specifically, autobiographical) in form. From this point of view 'to leave the story teller to himself' would be to leave Christian practice – unconstrained by historical literary and philosophical criticism – exposed to the risk, endemic to all autobiography, of 'self-indulgence and dishonesty' … There is thus a sense in which the indispensability of theology is the indispensability of criticism for all forms of ideology. (Lash 1986, pp. 117–18)

Subjectivity must be *critical* subjectivity, not treating our experiences, practices and prejudices as the yardstick of true understanding and practice, but interrogating them to expose what lies beneath, opening it to critical scrutiny. Tools of such interrogation have been: unearthing and acknowledging the role of autobiographical determinants in our understanding of the relationship between the Bible and life; identifying changes across time, and differences between us in our hermeneutical engagement; biblical criticism; theological conceptualization; historical analogues; and critical theoretical perspectives from human sciences.

The Bible itself offers to us a rich store of compelling (and repelling) stories, analogues, claims, images, examples, mysteries, riddles and invitations. As does all human life. In this process of critical reflection the Bible and human experience and practice are both the sources and both the objects of critique. The process of critical reflection is continuous and iterative, being thus a 'hermeneutical circle' which can be entered at any point, and in which the various parts, or particularities, illuminate the whole, and the whole illuminates the particulars. It is impossible to step out of this circle, though it is both possible and necessary to describe, however imperfectly, how we are managing the flux. To put this into a rather different discourse, if the first level of reflection is to interpret or give meaning to experience/practice/life/text (doing this, or describing how we have done this in the past, forms the bulk of Chapters 1–5), and the second is to reflect critically on how we have done that interpretation and reflection (we have to a certain extent interwoven this reflection with narratives, but focused explicitly on such critical reflection at the ends of these chapters and in the whole of Chapter 6), what we are doing in these final two chapters is the third level – asking what kinds of patterns of similarity or difference our interpretive strategies make. We thus engage in 'third order' reflection about our hermeneutical methodology.

We first identify patterns of similarity: living a critical human life, finding a critical and imaginative space, negotiating heteronomy and the ego, and putting ourselves on the page.

Living a critical human life

Reading the familiar words of Hebrews 4.12–13 in Nick King's translation of the New Testament we were struck by the appositeness of the words for so much of what we are seeking to articulate:

> For God's word is alive and powerful, and sharper than any two-edged sword; and it reaches as far as the point of division

of soul and spirit, of joints and marrows, and *it examines critically* [our italics] the reflections and thoughts of a heart. And nothing created is concealed before him: everything is naked and exposed to the scrutiny of the one to whom we have to give an account. (King 2004)

'Examining critically our reflections and thoughts' not only epitomizes the thesis of our book but also includes words that feature throughout it – examine, critical and reflection are the most obvious. But the language in 4.13, about nothing being concealed, and everything being made manifest and laid bare, echoes not only the words of that most apposite of prayers from the Book of Common Prayer which addresses God as the one 'from whom no secrets are hid', but also the 'unmasking' theme of 'apocalypse' with which our story begins.

That same Letter to the Hebrews offers us a compelling example of an author summoning readers to find a different space which might as a result offer a critical perspective on their lives: '[Jesus] suffered outside the gate. Therefore, let us go out to join him, outside the camp, bearing his reproaches (Heb. 13.13; King 2004, p. 560).

The spatial metaphor evoked by these words encapsulates what it is we are seeking to do. It is not that we can presume to have joined him, but we are seeking to do so, and that journey 'outside the camp' gives us the possibility of space where we can learn discernment of ourselves, our motives, failings and opportunities, as well as a critical view of the local and global society in which we live. This is how the Bible has had its part to play in our critical journey. We have learned that we are strangers and aliens, not quite fitting, living in the cracks, trying to be as at home as we can be in Babylon, while all the time struggling to know how we seek its welfare. As the author of the Letter to the Hebrews acknowledged, inhabiting that critical space might involve reproach; it is often no place of comfort or escape. What that journey outside the 'camp' involves encompasses the totality of the experience of life, and is not easily reduced to the rediscovery of the original meaning of the text, or to church doctrine.

Criticism is not an optional extra in life but is central to our humanity, 'as inevitable as breathing'. T. S. Eliot discusses the critical work of the human mind and claims that, whether we are conscious of doing so or not, whether we reflect on it or not, we all exercise some kind of critical function simply by virtue of being a human being, just as we all breathe (Eliot 1951).

Finding an imaginative and critical space

In our first two chapters we established the fundamental role that the Bible plays for us in furnishing an imaginative and critical space for us. Our critical and imaginative space is not solipsistic or self-absorbed, but is rooted in a 'cosmic' vision – one that embraces creation set free from its bondage to decay and the glorious freedom of the children of God (Rom. 8.21).

Criticism is not primarily about analytical and cognitive intelligence, but about a determined and committed reflective engagement which takes into account the needs of others and the structures that make their lives less fulfilled than they might be. What we have learned from Blake and Ruskin, and indeed many others, is that when the critical faculty becomes detached from engagement with life it risks doing exactly what Ernst

Käsemann (see Chapter 3, p. 52) said it would and becomes a barrier to our quest for self-reflexivity.

That mix of the horizon of hope, and the attention to the particularity of context and persons in that context, together provide the foundations and framework for reflective, critical space. In this the Bible is a means to an end. The richness and fruitfulness of the Bible do not stop for us with the original text, but are multiplied by the 'effective history' of this text in its reception and use over succeeding generations. The imaginative and critical space opened up by the biblical texts, which declare 'it shouldn't be like this' – or indeed 'it might be like that' – have enabled men and women, sometimes separated by centuries, to engage with an apocalyptic/eschatological perspective, which sheds light on the present. We have discussed some of them – Blake, Ruskin, Winstanley, Bonhoeffer, Liberation and Feminist theologians and others. The analogical method (Ashton 2000, pp. 6–28), which compares differing narratives, at different times and places, but all informed by this critical and imaginative horizon of hope, functions just as the Bible itself does to jolt us out of our complacency and taken-for-granted ideology to see that things might be/should be other than they are, and that the truth may look different from a different vantage point (Soskice 1993). Such comparisons, such seeing from a different perspective, raises a question mark over our contemporary life. What this means is that there is 'grit' in the shoe of life which makes one hesitate about being 'at ease in Zion' (cf. Amos 6.1). Issues that can be characterized by words like equality, need or freedom, however they may be construed in particular circumstances and in the lives of particular people, become central. The simple assertion 'it shouldn't be like this' for the majority of men, women and children raises the question: how have I and the society of which I am a part contributed to this sorry state of affairs?

The hermeneutical method at work here may be illustrated by what William Blake wrote about imaginative engagement and the central place that the Bible has in that process. In a rather tart response to a patron who was puzzled by Blake's images and wanted some kind of explanation Blake insisted that this is not what his work was about. Its function was, in imitation of 'the wisest of the ancients', to 'rouze the faculties to act'. What, in his estimation, was 'that which is not too explicit', which is 'the fittest for instruction'. He then lists biblical books alongside Aesop's Fables, Homeric epic and Plato in achieving this goal. He returns to the theme later in the letter and writes about the Bible, that it is 'more Entertaining & Instructive than any other book', as its contents 'are addressed to the Imagination ... & but mediately to the Understanding or Reason (Letter to Trusler 1799; E703).

This sentence, together with the words 'rouze the faculties to act', well sum up how it is that the Bible has functioned for us. We continue to be attracted to the Bible and find it instructive, not so much because it is Holy Writ but because we find that it has worked so well for us (as for countless others) in 'rouzing our faculties to act'. It has done this because, as Blake rightly points out, it has stimulated our imaginations and has helped in the process of critical reflection that we consider to be such an important part of what it is to be human. But, as Blake indicates, the order is crucial. Reason has its role but it does not come first. The Bible, Blake suggests, engages our imagination, our feelings and ourselves, and only then 'mediately' does reason get involved, with its own secondary contributory perspective on that initial imaginative engagement.

Blake's words in this context bear comparison with what he wrote about Jesus in *The Marriage of Heaven and Hell*: 'Jesus was all virtue; and acted from impulse: not from rules' (23–4, E40). George Eliot in *Silas Marner* (Chapter ii) wrote: 'he seemed to weave like the spider, from pure impulse, without reflection'. Unlike Silas Marner, Blake commends reflection but only after the initial imaginative engagement. The initial address to imagination followed by the mediation of reason encapsulates the thesis of our book. Blake's self-involving imaginative, creative engagement determines not only in his attitude to his more immediate predecessors Milton and Swedenborg, but in particular to the centrepiece of Christianity's tradition, the Bible. This is analogous to 'the great labour' of engaging with tradition, which T. S. Eliot wrote about:

> Yet if the only form of tradition, of handing down, consisted in following the ways of the immediate generation before us in a blind or timid adherence to its successes, 'tradition' should be positively discouraged. We have seen many such simple currents lost in the sand; and novelty is better than repetition. Tradition is a matter of much wider significance. It cannot be inherited, and if you want it you must obtain it by great labour. (Eliot 1951, p. 4; Prickett 2009, p. 210)

The language of detachment and critical space can justifiably conjure up images of the all too familiar 'holier than thou' attitude of traditional puritanical piety. The last thing we want to pretend is that we have got anything right and that the space we occupy is anything like 'holy'. We want to go on searching for an alternative space but one that is of absolute necessity perpetually negotiable and fragile and ever changing. As already noted, the emphasis on tolerance of difference comes out in passages like Romans 14 and possibly echoes Jesus' own words: 'Why do you pass judgment on your brother or sister? Or, you, why do you despise your brother or sister? For we will all stand before the judgment seat of God' (Rom. 14.10; cf. Matt. 7.1–3: 'Do not judge, so that you may not be judged. For with the judgment you make you will be judged, and the measure you give will be the measure you get. Why do you see the speck in your neighbour's eye, but do not notice the log in your own eye?'). Until the Last Judgement we 'see in a glass darkly' and only then 'face to face' (1 Cor. 13.12). Such practice not only complements being critical, but requires that love of neighbour. It means the abjuration of 'selfhood' and the recognition of 'the Other' in any situation.

Negotiating heteronomy and the ego

Both of us have been touched by movements in Christianity which give a prominent place to Scripture, which explains the fact that the Bible is in our bloodstream. But we do not believe that it should be given priority, as we seek to clear an imaginative space for ourselves (Bloom 1997, p. 5).

This question of priority is constantly debated within practical theology; does the Bible (or some other element of the Christian tradition) have a privileged place in the conversation between the self, the contemporary context and the tradition? Behind this lies the question of revelation. We have often found ourselves so near and yet so far from those who espouse a view of the Bible expressed in terms of the theology of Karl Barth. Thus Zoë in response to Richard Briggs' review of her *Using the Bible in Practical Theology*:

> Richard offers the view that the Barthian approach of starting with the revelation of God can more easily accommodate the significance of context, than starting with human context can accommodate the revelation of God. He rightly says that I did not make the opposite case, but rather suggested an interrelationship. He politely did not say this, but he would have been right had he said I want to muddy the waters a bit. Richard uses two expressions: 'a human framing of the context', and 'a theological account of a revealing God'. And herein lies the issue for me: why should we expect to meet the self-revelation of God any more through human theological accounts than through human accounts of experience and context? They are both human accounts. Is not the Bible itself a human account, taken to itself by human communities, in which we find human theological accounts and human accounts of experience and context? (Bennett in Briggs 2014, 7.6)

In the Introduction we distinguished ourselves from the position that Karl Barth takes about 'the strange new world within the Bible'. For us it is integral to the critical task. Indeed, we would go so far as to say it is indispensable. But our answer would not be primarily theological, in Barth's sense, at least not in the sense that the Bible is *the* encounter with God and so relativizes all else.

As we have suggested, liberation theology and feminist theology as well as the welter of experience of our lives, have been important components alongside the Bible in our search for a critically imaginative space where we can engage in reflection on our practice. That practice will be inspired by the Bible – but by much else too, not least patterns of human relating, those human encounters where what God means to us and calls us to is opened. It is a theological position we share with the liberationist hermeneutic and its emphasis on the encounter with the Son of Man in the poor, vulnerable and oppressed: 'Truly I tell you, just as you did not do it to one of the least of these, you did not do it to me' (Matt. 25.45). Passages like this point us beyond the covers of the Bible to where we shall meet Christ today. There is a sense in which any book that had the mix of enabling apocalypse and hope and wrestling with the discernment of life between the ages would have done as well as the Bible. But that is its genius. We share Blake's pragmatic belief that we have found the Bible to be the best there is because its component parts 'are addressed to the Imagination … & but mediately to the Understanding or Reason'. The process of practice and reflection is always experimental, because it is a journey, and as our ancestors in the New Testament bear witness, we are *in medias res.* Meanwhile 'we se in a glasse even in a darke speakynge' (1 Cor. 13.12, William Tyndale's translation).

We share Karl Barth's dissatisfaction with the adequacy of the biblical scholarship of his day fully to grasp what the biblical text is about without the self-involvement of the reader, so well exemplified in the following passage from his commentary on Romans:

> Intelligent comment means that I am driven on till I stand with nothing before me but the enigma of the matter; till the document seems hardly to exist as a document; till I have almost forgotten that I am not its author; till I know the author so well that I allow him to speak in my name and am even able to speak in his name myself. (Barth 1933, pp. 6–8)

Such a struggle to find ways of relating to the biblical (or any other older) text is a necessary part of any interpretation. 'The enigma of the matter' is reminiscent of Tyndale's translation of the Greek ἐν αἰνίγματι 'in a dark speakynge', a good way of characterizing the interpretative challenge. Where we would differ from Barth is that a crucial part of that process is that along with the Bible in negotiating the critical space, we must understand ourselves and how our context informs the way we interpret the Bible.

Tim Gorringe, who is as devoted to liberation theology as he is to the theology of Barth, has helpfully attempted to compare Barth and liberation theology and has pointed out the differences as well as the similarities. Indeed, he suggests that 'Barth has some claim to be a liberation theologian before his time' (1999, p. 269). But it is in beginning with human experience, a pervasive theme of this book, that Tim has pointed to a major difference from Barth:

> In the attempt to be faithful to the God who takes the side of the lowly, liberation theology committed itself to the priority of praxis and the 'true Church of the poor', so that for some

> practitioners, at least, the poor themselves became the bearers of the gospel and theology became reflection on praxis in itself. One can imagine how Barth would have reacted to such proposals: any theology which begins with human experience represents in his view, a return to the fleshpots of Egypt because some kind of ideological captivity is certain to be involved. (Gorringe 1999, p. 269)

Some much quoted words of Barth bear this out: 'take your Bible and take your newspaper, and read both. But interpret newspapers from your Bible' ('Barth in Retirement', *Time Magazine* 31 May 1963).

The problem is that there is *no* theology, no biblical exegesis, in which human experience is absent. We all have to engage with our embodied life. In one of his letters to Barth, Rudolf Bultmann took issue with him pointing out that 'philosophical fragments float in the soup of all theologians' (Jaspert 1982, p. 99). There is no escape, no resort to some transparent source of authority and guidance, to which we can give unambiguous assent, for there is no revelation that is compelling and authoritative; every one requires discernment (cf. 1 Cor. 14.26, 29). If we have learned anything from feminist theology, it is that the Bible as a collection of time-conditioned documents and the dogma that spawned it required as much careful ideological critique as that of any other institution. Barth is right to be suspicious of experience, but the same kind of suspicion is required of the Bible too. Even key theological terms like 'grace' need such a critique. The use of such words not least in human struggles is ideologically captive and there is no way to freedom apart from via a perpetual self-examination. There is no escape from ideology critique of some kind and the Bible does not offer an infallible guide to practice. The inspiration of Christoph Blumhardt whose life and work were so important for Barth characterizes so many of the views taken in this book:

> 'the unique element, and I say it quite deliberately, the prophetic, in Blumhardt's message and mission consists in the way in which the hurrying and the waiting, the worldly and the divine, the present and the coming, again and again met, were united, supplemented one another, sought and found one another'. Blumhardt was a man who 'believed in God and believed also in human beings, and because he believed in human beings believed also in the renewal of the world'. (Barth, quoted in Gorringe 1999, p. 289)

In the light of the never-ending task of discovering a critical space we question whether there is any real security in an external authority, whether Bible or Church, or the dominant institutions of society. It would be easy to say that we do submit ourselves to Christ but that assertion is itself not without problems – as do all claims to be obeying an authority outside and beyond ourselves.

What is the character of the demand that is laid upon us, and how can we be sure that the understanding of that demand is not infected by our powerful self-centeredness? It is the perennial problem of discernment that was already an issue in the New Testament. To take resort in a believing community only passes the buck as we see from history such communities are deeply divided. We believe there is no escape from the necessary and ever-observant self-criticism that we have tried to articulate, for heteronomy is no answer. Nor do we have access to a detailed checklist; it is more the art of recognizing the necessity of learning how best to 'love a brother or sister whom [we] have seen' and thereby 'love God whom [we] have not seen' (1 John 4.20).

This is not subordinating or even negating the self, but it is learning awareness of its insidious effects and finding ways of constraining it. Some words of Sister Edmée of the Sisters of the Love of God in an unpublished meditation put the point so well to those of us who would do good:

> it is precisely in becoming identified with a cause that one may betray it ... the ego is aroused and attaches itself to a particular cause ... it will then be the ego, now identified with this cause, which works on its behalf. Such identification is the antithesis of poverty of spirit, and these are its signs: it is elated by success, cast down by failure, enraged by criticism, sustained by self-righteousness. It engages in acrimonious controversy, does not restrain itself from scoring debating points, even in matters of life and death, and seizes even its sympathizers by the throat – down which it thrusts its message. Finally at the end of a very hard day, it retires into its corner sobbing with self-pity.

Self-interest pervades even the most noble acts of altruism; the recognition of this and of the extent to which such acts become an 'ego trip' are crucial for our flourishing.

Blake touches on the issue of awareness of the enormous pressure from the ego, to motivate action that is self-promoting rather than arising from poverty of spirit. By the end of *Jerusalem*, for example, the long road to redemption seems to have led nowhere, before things then change. The key is found in these words:

> Jesus said: 'Wouldest thou love one who never died/ For thee or ever die for one who had not died for thee /And if God dieth not for Man & giveth not himself/ Eternally for Man could not exist. for Man is Love: /As God is Love: every kindness to another is a little Death/ In the Divine Image nor can Man exist but by Brotherhood.' (*Jerusalem* 96.24–28, E256)

It is not just creative endeavour in building Jerusalem in this green and pleasant land that counts but *how* one does it. Embrace of the crucified Christ offers a paradigm for human beings and their relating. What Blake wrote is akin to what Winstanley described as 'the Wildernesse-condition', 'wherein a man is dead to all his owne wisdom, memory, strength, learning, actings, and looks upon all as priviledges of no gain, but of weaknesse and of drosse; without the *Anointing*, he cannot meditate, nor understand; till God come into him' (*The Breaking of the Day of God*, Corns, Hughes and Loewenstein 2009, i.140–1). Both Winstanley and Blake in their different ways echo themes from Pauline texts about the ethical significance of identification with the crucified Christ (for example, Rom. 6.3–11).

But espousal of the language of identification with the self-giving Christ is no antidote to lack of poverty of spirit. After all, 'Not everyone who says to me, "Lord, Lord," will enter the kingdom of heaven, but only the one who does the will of my Father in heaven' (Matt. 7.21). Being 'cast down by failure, enraged by criticism, sustained by self-righteousness', engagement 'in acrimonious controversy', may still happen. In this respect, there is much to learn from the Pauline letters. The Corinthian Christians may well have tried Paul's patience, but in his response, particularly in 2 Corinthians, he pulls rank, taking the theological high ground, as he presumes to offer himself as a type of Christ, the very embodiment of the crucified Christ (2 Cor. 4.10), a pattern that he expects the Corinthians to imitate (1 Cor. 11.1). The rhetoric of 2 Corinthians is a salutary warning about the way even the most sublime ethical theological language can be co-opted in the service of an exercise of self-justification and egotistical persuasion, however understandable it might have been.

The power struggle over language goes on. For example, language about 'formation' has become part of the common parlance in the context of Christian ministerial training. The import of a passage like Galatians 4.19 ('My little children, for whom I am again in the pain of childbirth until Christ is formed in you') is inclusive and less problematic than those passages where the pattern of the Christ is offered by Paul himself (e.g. 1 Cor. 4.16, 11.1; 2 Thess. 3.7, 9). When the pattern of Christ is intimately tied with his own persona, especially in passages in 2 Corinthians, it becomes an attempt to exercise power over others. As a result, a pattern of Christian existence is set up which means allowing oneself to be formed and moulded by what one has received, and even more problematically by the one who passes it on, in a passive, submissive and uncreative way.

What we have attempted to do in the preceding section is to locate ourselves in relation to a dominant strand of modern biblical theology, indicating our similarities to and difference from it. It is negotiating how on the one hand to acknowledge our great debt to the Bible, without on the other hand being in thrall to it. We too are inspired by the 'strange world' in the Bible but the authoritative heteronomous status it has been given is for us part of the problem, as it does not offer any solution to learning to live a reflective life in the world.

Putting ourselves on the page

Earlier in the book we outlined two ways in which we practised self-involving exegesis and the contrasting ways in which the Bible has been a part of our lives and contributed to our self-reflexivity. The relationship of our individual narratives and how they relate to the character of biblical narrative is explored in this last section of this chapter. We do this by considering story-telling and the importance of narrative in relation to the biblical engagement of the Ignatian Exercises, the growing recognition of the autobiographical character of biblical study, and auto-ethnography as a component of self-reflexivity, with reference to the history of biblical interpretation.

Story-telling

Throughout what we have written there is an emphasis on the self-involving interpreter. An important way in which we become 'involved' with both the 'text' of life and the 'text' of the Bible is through story. We want to share our stories, because we believe that the telling of stories is a crucial part of what makes us who we are and is a fundamental part of how it is we engage with our present and above all with texts, not least classic, authoritative texts like the Bible. The possibilities of engagement in a parabolic mode with the Bible are all the more exciting as what we have in the Bible is neither philosophy, nor neat doctrinal formulation, but page after page of story, in one form or another. To find ways in which these ancient stories, themselves the product of experience and the wrestling with disappointment and bewilderment, always tinged with hope, can illuminate, though not offer answers to, our own stories, and help us understand our experience of where we are now, is what this book is about. Our present, peculiar experiences are key, but experiences meditated upon and, as far as we can, understood in a variety of different ways.

'Experience has fallen in value', wrote Walter Benjamin in a thought-provoking essay from the 1930s on the storyteller and the demise of the significant role of experience, and the ways in which the communicability of experience is decreasing (1992, pp. 83–107). But, and this qualification is crucial, he rightly points out that 'counsel is less an answer to a question than a proposal concerning the continuation of a story which is unfolding'. The fossilization of story in a book, the novel being itself a product of a print culture, contrasts with the many-layered character of the story told over and over again. Novels too often have a moral message from the author, whereas the storyteller's narrative is told, and its reception and impact on the hearer will be less an answer and more an opportunity to engage with a story *in medias res.* As Benjamin puts it, 'it is half the art of story telling to keep a story from explanation', nor does it 'aim to convey the pure essence of the thing'. We might add, although Benjamin does not discuss this, that theory has become the way we understand texts, and in addition Christian doctrine has become an indispensable lens through which those who count themselves Christian are *required* to read the Bible narratives. What Benjamin writes touches on two crucial elements in the gospels which ought to be central to any Christian criticism. The first is that throughout these texts the heart of what constitutes pedagogy is tied up with stories and their impact on their readers/hearers, hence the frequent introduction 'With what can we compare the Kingdom of God' followed by a story or brief analogy (e.g. Mark 4.30).

Second, and notoriously, the same chapter of Mark's Gospel has the interpretative conundrum of the difference between those who *get* the message and those who don't, between insiders and outsiders, for whom everything is just stories, nothing more, and they may see but not perceive. Even those who begin to see find themselves accused by Jesus of not really perceiving what is going on (cf. Mark 8.21). But they have moved beyond the first step towards comprehending the next mode of understanding which is contingent on their *experience* of what they see (primarily) and what they hear. Once the first disciples have left their nets and followed Jesus they walk with him on the way and the slow process of understanding is intimately bound up with their experience 'on the way' (Mark 9.34, 10.32). None of this is about adherence to correct teaching so much as about what it means to them to follow, to go to Jerusalem, to accompany one who dared to challenge the hierarchy and paid the penalty of death. Indeed, Jesus himself, according to the Gospel of Mark at least, may not have fully understood how his vocation would work itself out. For these disciples, story, personal and Jesus' story, illuminated and understood and even explained by stories from life, together make up the dynamics of a self-aware, critical existence.

Narrative is by its very nature contextual. It tells a story of a particular time and place, and even then of more than one time and place as the narrative itself may betray the context of its author or redactor in the form in which the story is told. The biblical narratives have engaged audiences at many different times and places and in different ways. But it is the particularity of the context that is hermeneutically crucial. A story about another time and place is just that, time-bounded and reflecting different concerns from those of later readers.

Those later readers too have stories, indeed many stories, to tell and these are a necessary part of the interpretative process for anyone who wishes to engage with narratives from the past, however august and apparently sacrosanct. The latter cannot be applied without taking into account their particularity. The best way of doing this is to do justice to the particularity of the narratives of the later readers also. The necessity of negotiating a way of allowing the one narrative to inform the other in mutually illuminating ways is a crucial part of the critical process. This kind of method differs from the way in which concepts function as heuristic tools. A narrative cannot be an abstraction. It is about lives lived, interactions and sometimes about that which is incomplete and in the midst of things – complex, varied and resisting a neat summary. The medium is the message, and that means acknowledging and living with the complexity in the ways of telling a story.

Compare the gospel narratives with the Pauline letters. When Paul refers to Jesus, or Christ as he prefers to call him, he does so by reference to moments like the crucifixion or resurrection and the general characteristics such as his humility and obedience. What are lacking are the specifics of time and place and story. So what the Pauline presentation lacks is specificity and diachronicity, which are so typical of narrative texts and are two very distinctive characteristics of all the gospel portrayals. What we are offered instead (passages like 1 Cor. 11.23–25 apart) are certain *general* characteristics about Jesus, for example, his obedience unto death and his transformation, reflecting two aspects of the Jesus story, crucifixion and resurrection. But the specifics of how Jesus was obedient at a particular time and place, for example, are almost completely lacking. In this respect Paul's writings differ from the gospels.

What we are offered in the Pauline letters instead is an emphasis on Paul as a (*the*?) mediator of Jesus. So, Paul as agent of Jesus Christ communicated Christ's presence in his own person and behaviour, and especially in his letters, to those with whom he had to deal. This is one of the crucial elements of the Pauline understanding of presence and absence. How right Thecla was, according to the Acts of Paul 21, to have seen 'the Lord looking like Paul!' So there is the merging of present and past, either by neglecting or ignoring the specifics of Jesus' character and personality and life, how he was obedient and indeed how transformed, and concentrating instead on the general, less time-specific characteristics.

It is part of the genius of the early Christians that they chose narratives as the means whereby they understood themselves.

Doctrinal abstractions take second place to stories of a life, with all their variety. Engaging with such narratives beckons readers to relate these narratives to their own and wrestle with the enigmas that such a comparison throws up and the self-involving character of such reading, to which we now turn.

We have already had reason to mention *The Spiritual Exercises of Ignatius Loyola* in the context of cultivating self-reflexivity. But The Exercises also bring home the awareness that the biblical texts are a resource for exploration of what a life in its fullness may involve. So engagement with the Jesus story informs and subverts assumptions in every part of life. The way of engaging with the Bible promoted in The Exercises is at one and the same time an inspiration and a discomfort. The Ignatian tradition shows how the Bible can be part of a *self-reflective and critical* path, which may enable better understanding of the world and the God who is met in those around us and our interactions with them. Implicitly imaginative insertion of the reading subject into the gospel narrative means s/he brings a welter of experience, possibly not formally constructed into a narrative though having rudimentary outlines as memory and development, which lend a diachronic perspective to the variety of incidents. Biblical exegesis is an arcane activity but is in principle open to anyone. It demands a degree of self-awareness of the variety of factors that determine one's quest for understanding. The Exercises open up exploration of our interests (economic, political, philosophical as well as religious) that we bring to the text. Understanding them is a necessary part of developing a critical awareness. Where exegesis of any kind (whether carried out in an academic environment or not) is viewed merely as a theoretical enterprise cut off from our wider context in a world dominated by poverty and suffering, important ingredients will be lacking.

Autobiography, autoethnography and reflection on the self

Critical interpretation is interpretation that makes explicit the particular interpretive processes and choices of evidence through which it constructs meaning in a text. This then opens the possibility for an assessment on theological and moral grounds of the relative value of this interpretation as compared with other interpretations. A critical interpretation will include understanding of the contextuality of one's pedagogical formation, as well as one's psychological and socio-economic interests. This is an approach to knowledge which we name 'critical subjectivity'. Instead of 'objectivity' which is impossible, and the claim to which always distorts knowledge, 'critical subjectivity' invites critical scrutiny of the autobiographical – for both the positive generation of knowledge and for the attention to ways in which the knowing subject may distort the knowledge.

The biblical interpreter and writer on hermeneutics, Daniel Patte, has rightly attempted to tease out the reasons for academic suspicion of the autobiographical character of interpretations among biblical scholars (Patte 2002). He suggests that the practice of biblical scholars is framed by a quest for universal and objective conclusions about 'what the text meant' that they posit as the necessary basis for any formulation of 'what the text means'. In the light of their assumptions, an autobiographical reading cannot be critical, because it is subjective. Despite the lip service paid to hermeneutics and the inevitability of 'pre-understanding', the quest is always on for an interpretation that has a higher degree of probability than others. Inserting the interpreting self into criticism is considered an impossibility because there seems to be no objective way to assess what are greater or lesser degrees of probability in subjective interpretation.

Patte advocates a practice of autobiographical biblical studies free from the subject/object dichotomy, and from a view of 'meaning' as something that exists apart from interpretation:

- any interpretation of a biblical text, including the most rigorous technical analysis, is autobiographical – it is framed by pre-understandings;
- diverging interpretations involve distinctive interpretive choices that reflect their respective autobiographical characters; and therefore, that
- a comparison aimed at identifying the distinctive interpretive choices made, by contrast with those made in other interpretations, reveals the autobiographical character of interpretation.

So there is something to learn from diverging interpretations which may bring forth neglected features of the text.

The major types of interpretative choice that give any interpretation its autobiographical character are: *autonomy* (the selection of particular exegetical or analytical methods), *contextual relational choices* (the interpreter's place in a life-context, which includes a web of social and power/authority relations), and *heteronomy* (that includes coming to the text with certain theological concepts that reflect the interpreters' positive or negative religious experiences including experiences of the silence or absence of God). These interpretive choices are important. For Patte, being critical involves making explicit the autobiographical character of one's interpretation, the interpretative *choices*, which include analytical, contextual, and hermeneutical-theological choices, and how these choices frame one's interpretation. A comparison with the interpretative practice of others is a crucial aid in elucidating the variety of interpretative choices, not least those made by oneself. This book reflects the kind of interpretative choices that Daniel Patte mentions. Our interpretative methods are those of historical study of the Bible, *throughout history* not just the period of the genesis of the biblical books, and the mainstream methods of practical theology. These are evident throughout. We have attended to our particular existential and professional contexts, at least indirectly if not in detail, especially in Chapters 3 and 4, and our theological basis is set out in Chapters 3 and 6 in particular.

Such attention to autobiography is closely allied to the process involved in autoethnography. Both involve seeking, understanding and representing knowledge through attention to the self, and the position of the self in a social context. Much of this book has affinities with an autoethnographic method. We have, especially and explicitly in Chapters 1, 3 and 4, sought to derive knowledge and understanding through asking *how we did in practice* use/relate to the Bible in the context of our lives, and in the wider context of the communities we inhabited. The critical interrogation of the self in context is the heart of the autoethnographic method. It works with what is the case 'in practice' rather than what ought to be the case ideally, that is 'in thought'.

Autoethnography is commonly characterized as 'evocative', 'analytic' or 'performance' (Walton 2014, pp. 4–9). Our writing has elements of all three. It is evocative in that the telling of our stories, including the emotional and affective elements, leads us, and we hope the reader, into a holistic understanding that is in part prompted by recognition, the gestalt moment of 'aha!' We 'seek to speak out of epiphanic moments of transformation' in a way that acknowledges complexity and ambiguity, and enables 'deeper perceptions to emerge' (p. 5).

Our autoethnographic writing seeks to be analytic in the sense that the stories we tell form the basis for an analysis of our critical hermeneutical method, and beyond that for an examination of the patterns of similarity and difference in our hermeneutical methods. Such analysis also engages with the wider context of communities of readers of the Bible, the academic and church communities to which we have belonged, and their own situatedness within a cultural context. The analytic autoethnographic approach is a way to 'investigate and theorize about the social world' (p. 6); our stories, and our descriptions of how in practice we *do* interpret the Bible and employ it as a means to live a critical human life, lead us into processes of reflection, comparison, questioning and the discovery of imaginative spaces which enable a form of theory-building.

Our writing is performance autoethnography in two senses. It recalls and articulates the performances of our lives – preaching sermons, writing academic essays, travelling (literally) to places of new insight and finding strategies for living. It is also in itself a 'performance' through which we have learned to understand better the subject matter we write about. A significant part of 'performing' the writing of this book has been the collaborative nature of the work.

Personal narratives in the context of interpretation

If we examine the archaeology of our Bible reading, we both have led a hermeneutical double life in which we have been exposed to the 'self-involving' and the 'detached' ways of reading and in different ways over the years these have become part of our hermeneutical history. One doesn't have to choose between them; the issue is about being critical. Our problem with much current biblical criticism is not that it is too critical, but that it is not critical enough.

The induction into academic ways of reading biblical texts tends to involve keeping the interpreting self out of the process. But that in turn means the adoption of a particular hermeneutical strategy hammered out in the early modern period, which has gained hegemonic status now, in which a particular form of historical reading holds sway. The briefest glance at the history of hermeneutics indicates that it was not ever thus. Rather what we have now is probably the end of a phase in biblical interpretation, whose critical purchase is trumpeted but is in fact limited. The problem is, therefore, that the preoccupation with the quest for the original meaning/ authorial intention is a symptom of a particular hermeneutical phase and set of preoccupations, which often includes ensuring that the interpreting subject is bracketed out (see Frei 1974; Rowland

2016). The consequence has been a uniform kind of interpretation, deemed 'objective', as a bulwark against individualism and the vagaries of experience. It has become the *sine qua non* of reading and the gold standard of counting as critical.

Criticism is an ever-changing quest for a critical space which is going to be as varied as the individuals and communities who practice it. What we have slowly discovered through our exposure to liberation and feminist theology and our 'cloud of witnesses' is that criticism is not just about detachment and the narrow form of historicism that typifies most modern academic engagement with the Bible, but about the interests (intellectual, economic and personal) involved in becoming part of and maintaining any hermeneutical system. It is not our belief that historical enquiry as an intellectual task is unnecessary and should be dispensed with, but that it is inadequate. It is inadequate as a response to texts that demand involvement, even if that involvement is negative and questioning. The nature of criticism is altogether more complicated and exciting, not least precisely because it makes explicit and wrestles with background and prejudices of individuals and communities.

Hans-Georg Gadamer is one of the great pioneers of modern hermeneutics (Gadamer 1979). Gadamer's intellectual legacy gets us to take on board the fact that experience and culture influence biblical study. There are inevitable cultural influences on the interpreter; the recognition must be there that even the supposedly most scientific exegesis is contextual, rooted in its tradition of interpretation, whether it is acknowledged or not. Biblical scholars can benefit from the application of self-reflexivity, for the supposedly detached observations are not independent of the researcher. Experience and culture inform and illuminate understanding, which raises the issue of self-involvement in reading the Bible. Our reactions to a text are an essential part of the hermeneutical mix.

It is intellectual impoverishment to exclude our involvement and responses to texts and emphasize scholarly detachment solely. The Bible is not just an object of study but engages the interpretative subject. In oft-quoted words from 'Confessions of an Inquiring Spirit' (1840) Samuel Taylor Coleridge wrote: 'In my last letter I said that in the Bible there is more that *finds* me than I have experienced in all other books put together' (Coleridge in Hart 1956, p. 43). Herein lies a dimension of ancient and indeed modern biblical usage, in which engaging critically with self-involvement in the process of interpretation is key. What is needed is the cultivation of a critical awareness, enabling people to see how they are reading the Bible. To be critical is to be human, and this requires us to be aware of our prejudices. The process of negotiating a critical space to reflect on what is both life giving and problematic is at the heart of life in the contemporary world, whether we are orthodox Christians or secular scholars. Being aware of one's interpretative predilections is not some optional extra, but the very stuff of critical exegesis. One can be immersed in the Bible while at the same time recognizing the difficulty of seeing it as a handbook for everyday living. The subtle interplay between ancient and modern context, experience and traditions of interpretation, and critical reflection are at the heart of the hermeneutical process. The way the Bible has been read, understood and interpreted in a variety of media in different contexts, and by people of very different backgrounds, orthodox and heretical, mainstream and marginal, has enabled these texts not only to be a means of life, in ways that their authors could never have dreamt of, but also a rich resource for the history of the understanding of one of the classic texts of Western culture.

Conclusion

In this chapter we have identified four key movements which pervade our interpretation of both life and the Bible. It is no coincidence that they are all expressed in verbal form: living, finding, negotiating and putting. Criticism is an activity; and it happens in the swirling vortex of communal human life. It never stands still, and it never happens in a vacuum.

The four movements are not cumulative, they do not happen in an order or in stages. However, in terms of our argument, finishing with 'putting ourselves on the page' does make explicit what we have already been talking about in the first part of this chapter in terms of finding a critical space and not opting for easy options (like heteronomy). So the 'heterogeneous' items all point to a central key point – the inescapability of self-involvement in all interpretation.

This chapter has plotted the patterns of similarity in our critical and interpretative strategies. The following chapter will open up some of the differences that exist in tension with the similarities and resist, as we said at the beginning of this chapter, any resort to a simple hermeneutical model.

8
The Owl of Minerva – a Retrospect

In the Venn diagram (p. 4) used in the Introduction one of the three key components was the idea of collaborative authorship. Whereas in the last chapter we traced patterns of similarity in the way we interpret the Bible and the way in which we relate life and the Bible together, this final chapter will explore cross currents that will resist any smooth flow, or to change the metaphor, any fixed models. These cross currents have arisen for us not only as we have seen how we relate the Bible and life differently, but also in the very action of writing the book. Practice and action disclose those similarities and dissimilarities. The chapter will begin with a focus on modes of biblical interpretation and move through them to the actual collaborative tasks of writing itself, and it will become clear that these two cannot be separated. The material of this chapter can be encapsulated in three words: mediation; metaphor and movement.

Mediation

What struck us both was that the nature of our self-involving reading is different. For one of us (C) it offers a kind of autobiographical language whereas for the other (Z) it is more detached, less first-hand.

The contrast is important. What comes across in Christopher's writing about Babylon in Chapter 4 is not mediation, for it is all very *im*-mediate. It is as if there is a sharing of the experience of Daniel and his colleagues, without any presumption to historical accuracy about what it must have been like. It was about affinity with the lives of aliens as they struggled with the hostile environment of the Babylonian court and tried to find a way to survive.

When Blake scribbled in the margin of one of his books 'The Beast and the Whore rule without controls' he captures this mind-set. The Bible offers access to a language, a way of being and seeing, albeit initiated through experience, which then helps to interpret the world. It is a ready and necessary resource to express in words the deepest feelings and apprehension of things when words seem to fail. Of course, in the process, the Bible is much less like a stern judge standing over against us, and more a necessary companion on the way. The crucial issue is whether such a process helps in living life, particularly in informing and enabling us to love our neighbours as ourselves.

So for Christopher it seems that there is no space between experience and its expression in biblical language, no kind of insertion of qualification, no hesitation, no obligation to detach oneself from it (at least initially), no doubt about the propriety of using the Bible in this way. It is a medium with which to make sense of feelings and fears – words trying to get at that which is beyond words, and it provides a metaphorical language to make sense of the chaos and confusion.

For Zoë, the Bible is mediated. This is shown clearly in Chapter 4, as the raising of Lazarus is given meaning in a sermon through the experiences of contemporary life, or in Chapter 3 experiences of Church and family life are illuminated not immediately by the Bible but mediately through theological and exegetical analysis. Such mediations may be evocative and emotional as well as analytical and cognitive. Her first understanding of resurrection came via C.S. Lewis's depiction of Lucy and Susan riding clinging on to the mane of the resurrected Aslan in *The Lion, the Witch and the Wardrobe*, which became the substance of the most joyful dreams and waking fantasies.

Metaphor

Two key images of how we relate to the Bible are having 'the Bible in our bloodstream' and of the Bible being part of 'the house of authority'. Playing with these images yields some ways of understanding our different approaches. 'The Bible in the bloodstream' is an ambiguous image that captures our similarities and our differences. We have both gladly used the image 'in the bloodstream' positively, but need to recognize that there are two aspects of the bloodstream which may help a little to tease out the difference in the use of the Bible in the two accounts. The bloodstream is that which constitutes each of us as living beings. So to assert that 'it is in our bloodstream' makes the point that it is constitutive of who we are and without it we could not exist. That comes out more clearly perhaps in the evocation of life in Babylon. Its model is the way the dying Jesus according to the Gospel of Mark turns to the Bible, and quotes Psalm 22, 'My God, my God, why have you forsaken me?' (Mark 15.34), *in extremis* to provide a way of expressing his deepest feelings of utter perplexity and destitution.

On the other hand our blood also contains crucial antibodies that are part of our immune system and protect our bodies against infections. It is that which is also there in the bloodstream, and that which resists the pathological items in one's body, that helps tease out the difference between the two approaches to the Bible taken in Chapter 3. In one case it is as if the Bible is the oxygen that keeps us alive; in the other it is inbuilt resistance to being taken over. One is characterized by that which enables existence through the flow of blood through the body. The other is about resisting that which damages that existence. Zoë's use of the Bible in Chapter 4 involves resistance precisely because the Bible was so much part of the 'house of authority' that was so oppressive. It was less a place of asylum and more a prison. Such experience pervades everything. The Bible may be used but doesn't as it were take one over. The two complement each other and indeed are necessary. There is an absolute necessity of the process of *resistance*, which is encapsulated by critical reflection. It is an antidote to help us deal with that which may be in our bloodstream or even help us understand what kind of house authority we may inhabit.

There was a revealing moment in the first piece that we co-authored. Christopher had written about liberation theology and had implicitly used it as a way of 'redeeming' the Bible. Zoë complemented that by saying that while much that was positive had emerged from a liberationist perspective, there was still an enormous problem posed by the Bible (Bennett and Rowland 2005). Feminist criticism has demonstrated that despite the variety of the Bible's cultural situations, they are all determined by the perspectives of a male-dominated society. That basic fact, informed by the wisdom of experience, is crucial. It is an essential component of having the 'Bible in the bloodstream', enabling resistance as well as positive engagement. Exposure to liberation theology and the centrality of contextual theology were not enough. It was also necessary to recognize the problems that the Bible itself posed. These were prior to the ways in which generations of Christians, inspired by mainly male interpreters, had understood it and from whose clutches many recent apologists for a 'politically sound' Bible (of whom Christopher now recognizes he was one!) have sought to loosen it.

The expression 'the house of authority' is taken from the work of Edward Farley. He describes the collapse of the house of authority, by which expression he indicates that the authoritative function of scripture within Christian faith means that people are seen primarily as people of the book, and so always under the tyranny of those institutional powers that mediate Scripture to the ordinary members of the people of God. It makes Christians captive to scriptures in a way that should not have happened to a people whose founding moment was when the Spirit was poured out on all flesh (Farley 1982).

Chapter 3 (Turning Points) describes the ways in which Zoë gained some critical distance from a particular manifestation of that house of authority she had taken on board, in its religious and sociological features, from the moment of explicitly embracing Christian faith in her teens. The explicitly religious and the (at the time) more widely accepted social values reinforced one another to produce an ideology from which it was extremely difficult to break. It seems highly likely that this particular set of circumstances has been instrumental in determining the kind of way Zoë has come to relate to the Bible. Her story of leaving, and finding critical distance from, the house of authority in which the Bible was a crucial instrument of maintaining a particular ideological world-view, has enabled her to activate the necessary 'antibodies'. These predispose her to a mediated understanding of the Bible, rather than the kind of trust in it that is indicated by the evangelical expression 'sitting under the text'. While 'sitting under the text' implies a heteronomy neither of us would find helpful (Chapter 7), it also inoculated her against the sort of immediate inhabiting of the text which Christopher described as essentially part of his own way of living with the Bible.

A source that has been a fruitful and inspiring resource for us both over the years is Latin American liberationist biblical hermeneutics, particularly as set out by Clodovis Boff (Boff 1987, pp. 142–50; cf. Bennett 2007, pp. 39–54). Boff contrasts two ways of engaging with the Bible in liberationist hermeneutics. The first is the immediate engagement ('correspondence of terms') where the modern reader identifies with a biblical story and the person or event in the Bible offers an imaginative frame for the modern world. The reader identifies with characters in the biblical stories. So, they become a way of speaking about and indeed understanding of, for example, displacement and homelessness or the experience of being people struggling for justice. The biblical stories are reflected *directly* in the experiences, in the case of the *comunidades eclesiais de base* in Brazil, of displacement, poverty, and powerlessness. It is an approach that has many similarities with the kind of interpretation we find in the New Testament (e.g. 1 Cor. 10.11). The words of the Bible become less a window onto antiquity and more a way of understanding oneself which are socially and contextually meaningful, something that the Velázquez image on the cover of the book enables also. The process is what Blake describes when he writes of the Bible being 'addressed to the Imagination which is Spiritual Sensation & but mediately to the Understanding or Reason' (Letter to Trusler, E703).

Subjective and imaginative engagement with the Bible is followed by critical reflection as reason takes a secondary, even if important, place to imagination. That secondary, reflective space is well brought out in Boff's other method ('correspondence of relationships'). In it one looks at the correspondence between the biblical text that bears witness to the life and struggles of the people of God at a particular time and place and one's contemporary context, the modern 'text of life'. Thus, there are two corresponding contexts that need to be kept in mind, the meaning of the text now and the hypothetical meaning of the text 'back then'. So, the understanding of the contemporary situation takes full account of the insights of sociology, psychology and politics, economics and power relations, and the same applies to the understanding of the text in its ancient context, which may inform, inspire and challenge modern readers of the Bible. There is some ambiguity about the relative priority between text and experience in what Boff writes. According to Boff, 'the thrust of the hermeneutic movement comes from scripture' (Boff 1987, pp. 150–1; noted by Bennett 2007, pp. 44–5). In his diagrammatical encapsulation of this method, Boff suggests that in the dialectical relationship between experience and text the former may act as a heuristic device to help illuminate what is the nature of that ancient situation to which the Bible bears witness: the hermeneutical equation drawn does not 'travel a one-way street', or 'read from left to right', from scripture to ourselves. The relationship is circular, like any genuine hermeneutic relationship. One might speak of a 'dialectical hermeneutic' (Boff 1987, p.149).

For Boff in 'the hermeneutic circle' of modern life and the persons and events to which the biblical texts bear witness there is a 'free play' of interpretation as 'meaning ... comes to light, in historical currency through and beyond the letter of the text of the past' (p. 148). The method he outlines is not a quest for formulas to 'copy' or techniques to 'apply' from Scripture. It does not presuppose the application of a set of principles to modern situations. Rather the Bible offers orientations, models, types and inspirations – elements permitting us to acquire, on our own initiative, a 'hermeneutic competency', the capacity to judge – on our own initiative, in our own right – 'according to the mind of Christ', or 'according to the Spirit', the new unpredictable situations with which we are continually confronted. The Bible, therefore, offers us 'not a *what*, but a *how* – a manner, a style, a spirit' (p. 149).

This is not the only way in which the analogical method can function. In this book, we reflect on the ways in which other sources, whether literary or iconographic, may help us to see better. Ruskin and Blake have been important for us, and we have set out to describe why and what we have learned from them for the ways we read the Bible. In fact, Boff's 'correspondence of relationships' method can embrace a variety of modes of understanding where the present can be illuminated and offer a critical perspective on how and who we are.

Movement

It is only at the end of the path that the journey is seen; and then the journey itself appears indistinguishable from the goal. As the great philosopher Hegel observed, the Owl of Minerva, the owl of wisdom, only takes its flight at dusk. It is a wonderful metaphor for the fact that only at the end of writing a book does one begin to see what has been learned in the writing of it. So it is no accident that a key feature for the conceptual framework of this book is the *practice* of collaborative authorship. Critical distance is activated in particular by discerning that someone else does not see from the same vantage point. Another person may not see in anything like the same way. In writing a book together it is essential always to remain open to another way of seeing what is going on.

So in this final section of the book we look at the process of collaboration which reveals a deeper understanding of how we actually do relate the Bible and life to each other than either of us had when we started, about the differences between us as well as the similarities. Sandra Gilbert and Susan Gubar's description of their collaboration on a book rings true for us too: 'reading metaphors in this experiential way, we have inevitably ended up reading our own lives as well as the texts we study, so that the process of writing this book has been … transformative … And much of the exhilaration of writing has come from working together' (Gilbert and Gubar 2000, p. xiii). For us as for them, this exhilaration of writing has come from working together and discovering greater understanding both of our own ways of interpreting life and the Bible, and also of the myriad ways in which such interpretations are possible. A deeper understanding of the inner also brings a deeper understanding of the outer.

Our work together over the years, combined with our experience of collaborative research and writing with colleagues, has shown us the importance of this way of working, in which the interaction of differing gifts has underlined the indispensability of the intellectual dialectic that such work entails. That necessarily includes being as honest as possible about the significant differences in the approach to research and writing.

Christopher finds the thesis through writing, which itself can involve disparate pieces of prose loosely related, which is based on hunches and intuitions reflected upon, largely from a personal point of view, and only subsequently related to secondary literature. From that, slowly, a thesis emerges. Zoë also finds the thesis through writing, but her process of writing is focused on the reader. She finds her voice as a speaker not as a writer, and she finds clarity for herself when writing as if she is speaking and explaining to others. This embeds the ordering and arrangement of material (secondary material included) in the process of writing from the very start. Negotiating those differences and harnessing them for the wellbeing of the project has been time-consuming but also very fulfilling. The alternating moments of insight and creativity and the various attempts at consolidation and keeping hold of the overall thesis of the book have been a shared enterprise.

There are significant differences in temperament and approach within the context of a shared commitment to a theology that is both practice-based and necessarily attentive to experience. One of us is more impulsive, with (perhaps too many!) new ideas to follow up. But that is complemented by the creative organization of the other. It is a skill so similar to creativity in music where the arrangement of notes, rhythm, harmony and counterpoint takes on a deliberately mechanical but extraordinarily creative and original flair as that which both holds the piece together as it takes shape and enables it to emerge as more than just a collection of notes on a page. Over the years, including in the title of an article we co-authored and in the Festschrift that Zoë co-edited for Christopher, we have found ourselves drawn to Gerrard Winstanley's words 'action is the life of all' ('A Watch-Word to the City of London', Corns, Hughes and Loewenstein 2009, ii.8).

What is essential not only for the interpretation of a drama or a piece of music is the performance of the words or the notes on the page. As Nicholas Lash has put it, 'the fundamental form of the interpretation of Beethoven consists in the performance of his texts' (Lash 1986, p. 41).

The act of writing collaboratively is a much-needed antidote to our shortcomings and fallibility, though there is no guarantee that collaboration will not turn into a collusion that will mask these from us. The process is dialogical and mutual, one offering a suggestion – an alternative way of saying or organizing things – and the other responding. From this process clarity of meaning and a coherence of presentation emerges which would not have come to one of us working alone. It is that kind of interchange at the practical level, added to the dialectic over the thesis of the book and the shape of its chapters, which has given the book the shape it has, and helped us to find some measure of critical space within the process. What started as a disparate set of pieces, directed in one way or another to our concerns, slowly evolved into a more coherent narrative as the result of the ongoing exchange about the nature and purpose of the book.

It would be presumptuous to write that we intended to model

what we have written about in the book in terms of critical reflexivity, though we hope we have begun to do that. In retrospect, however, this method has been an ever-evolving process of critical reflexivity considerably facilitated by joint authorship. We don't think of ourselves as pioneers, but we do testify to the importance to the development of a critical perspective that joint authorship brings. Jonathan Wolff wrote sympathetically about joint authorship and its relative rarity in humanities research and writing. We have valued the fact that 'one's ego gets submerged when writing with another person' (Wolff 2016). In a sense what collaboration does is ensure that peer review is a diachronic process throughout the genesis and gestation of the book not a discrete moment in its assessment.

In the Venn diagram at the beginning of the book (p. 4) we sought to describe the overlapping concerns between the Bible and the Christian tradition, our experience, both personal and professional, and the process of collaborative authorship, which in the later stages of writing has become an essential part of the conceptual framework. All together have contributed to the journey of discovery of what it means to live a 'reflective life'. We have written much about attempting to find a 'critical space'. Archimedes said, 'give me a place to stand on and I will move the world'. Yes, we need to stand back, but this is *not* the same as being 'objective' rather than 'subjective'. What is important is *critical* subjectivity. It is about finding a perspective from which we can see more than our immediate prejudices, learn more than we know already. Our quest to be critical has been to allow theory and practice to inform each other.

In a glass darkly: the Bible, reflection and everyday life

Our professional lives are also our 'everyday lives', and to pick up words from Michael Banner's recent book much of it 'goes without saying' (2014, pp. 201–2). Rightly, he points to the contribution of social anthropology and ethnography to help us notice and understand. One recent academic development, in which Zoë is much involved, is the professional doctorate in Practical Theology (DProf). It requires an intellectual reflection on one's professional life and the articulation of an appropriate critical space, in which the involvement of the interpreting subject is crucial. This requires the use of a variety of tools to clarify a method, which will enable the topic to be explored adequately, and a contribution to knowledge to be offered. While we didn't set out to write a textbook for those engaged in professional doctorates, our book has involved a very similar kind of intellectual reflection on our experience, personal and professional. As such it may make a contribution to those engaged in this exciting intellectual venture, as they seek to understand themselves better in their contexts.

For both of us there is a sense of bearing witness to a different way of looking at, and doing, things in our professions, to which life and the Bible together have contributed. We believe that it is the great contribution of much modern theology practised and written about from a liberationist perspective that its practitioners have challenged the rigorous exclusion of the interpreting subject from the process of reflection and shown how detached it is from strands of the Christian tradition including the Bible. Our lives have been illuminated by this way of engaging with our intellectual tradition. As we reflect on our professional lives we have found that the image of 'living in the cracks', has resonated with us. When John Bowker writes of transcending the protected or closed circle (2016, p. 162), we find that encapsulates so much of what we have sought to do in our professional lives as we have explored ways of being true to what we believe in contexts that have not always seemed conducive to the practice of those convictions. Nevertheless, *mutatis mutandis,* we have found ourselves following the advice of Jeremiah to seek the welfare of the city you dwell in. It explains why we continue to wrestle with Paul's contextual theology, even if we would not agree with all he recommends. For us contextual theology has involved a critical view on our institutional situations, where we have never felt totally at home but have still found cracks in which to flourish.

What may cause surprise is the inclusion of such a substantial role for the Bible in the process of self-reflexivity, indeed, in the process of critique more generally, when it has itself been the object of much criticism over the last 200 years. We have not denied the problems we have with the Bible but have seen its apocalyptic and eschatological perspective as a key part in the critical process that we deem to be the very stuff of existence. That strand in the Bible, along with others that complement it, has been crucial to the cultivation of a critical perspective, and we find it difficult to imagine ourselves developing a critical spirit, which is also affirming and informative without it. To return to those words of T. S. Eliot, which we quoted in the Introduction, the Bible has helped us decongest our critical airways as we have learned to engage in that which 'is as inevitable as breathing'.

Bibliography

Ashton, J., 2000, *The Religion of Paul the Apostle*, New Haven and London: Yale University Press.

Ashton, J., 2007, *Understanding the Fourth Gospel*, 2nd edn, Oxford: Clarendon.

Ashton, J., 2014, *The Gospel of John and Christian Origins*, Minneapolis: Fortress.

Banner, M., 2014, T*he Ethics of Everyday Life: Moral Theology; Social Anthropology and the Imagination of the Human*, Oxford: Oxford University Press.

Barrington, D., Bennett, Z. and Wymer, R., 2014, '"I was in love with both, so they could teach me anything": Ted Hughes, Pauline Mayne and Mexborough', *The Ted Hughes Society Journal* 4.1, pp. 119–28.

Barth, K., 1933, *The Epistle to the Romans,* Oxford: Clarendon.

Barth, K., 1935, *The Word of God and the Word of Man*, London: Hodder and Stoughton.

Benjamin, W., 1992, *Illuminations*, edited with an introduction by Hannah Arendt, London: Fontana.

Benjamin, W., 1992, 'The Storyteller: Reflections on the Works of Nikolai Leskov', in H. Arendt, ed., *Illuminations*,

London: Fontana, pp. 83–107.

Benn, T. 2004, *Dare to be a Daniel: then and now*, London: Arrow.

Bennett, Z., 2002, *Introducing Feminist Perspectives on Pastoral Theology*, Sheffield: Sheffield Academic Press.

Bennett, Z. and Rowland, C., 2005, 'Contextual and Advocacy Readings of the Bible', in Ballard, P. and Holmes, S., eds, *The Bible in Pastoral Practice: Readings in the place and function of scripture in the church*, London: Darton, Longman & Todd, pp. 174–90.

Bennett, Z., 2007, '"Action is the Life of All": The Praxis-Based Epistemology of Liberation Theology', in Rowland, C., ed., *The Cambridge Companion to Liberation Theology*, 2nd edn, Cambridge: Cambridge University Press, pp. 39–54.

Bennett, Z., 2008, '"To be Taught to See is to Gain Word and Thought at Once": John Ruskin and Practical Theology', *Practical Theology* 1.1, pp. 65–83.

Bennett, Z., 2011, '"To See Fearlessly, Pitifully": What does John Ruskin have to Offer to Practical Theology?' *International Journal of Practical Theology* 14.2, pp. 189–203.

Bennett, Z. and Gowler, D., eds, 2012, *Radical Christian Voices and Practice: Essays in Honour of Christopher Rowland*, Oxford: Oxford University Press.

Bennett, Z., 2013, *Using the Bible in Practical Theology: Historical and Contemporary Perspectives*, Aldershot: Ashgate.

Bennett, Z., 2016, 'Finding a Critical Space: Scripture and Experience in Practical Theology' in A. Paddison, ed., Theologians on Scripture, London: Bloomsbury, pp. 23–36.

Berger, P., 1967, T*he Sacred Canopy: Elements of a Sociological Theory of Religion*, New York: Doubleday

Blake, W., Access to images of Blake's illuminated books, the watercolor versions and Illustrations of the Book of Job, and some of his pictures of the Bible are available online at The William Blake Archive, www.blakearchive.org/blake/

Blake, William, ebook 1988, T*he Complete Poetry and Prose of William Blake*, edited by David V. Erdman, Berkeley, CA: University of California Press, available at www.english.uga.edu/~nhilton/Blake/blaketxt1/home.html. (References in the form of E followed by page number.)

Bloch, E., 1986, *The Principle of Hope*, Oxford: Blackwell.

Bloch, E., 2009, *Atheism in Christianity: The Religion of the Exodus and the Kingdom*, London: Verso.

Bloom, H., 1997, *The Anxiety of Influence*, 2nd edn, New York; Oxford: Oxford University Press.

Boff, C., 1987, *Theology and Praxis: Epistemological Foundations*, Maryknoll: Orbis.

Bonhoeffer, D., 1965, *No Rusty Swords*, London: Collins.

Bonhoeffer, D., 1981, *Letters and Papers from Prison*, London: SCM Press.

Bowker, J. W., 2016, *Why Religions Matter*, Cambridge: Cambridge University Press.

Bretherton, L., 2010, *Christianity and Contemporary Politics: The Conditions and Possibilities of Faithful Witness*, Chichester: Wiley-Blackwell.

Briggs, R., 2014, review of Bennett, Z., *Using the Bible in Practical Theology: Historical and Contemporary Perspectives, in Theology and Ministry* 3.7, pp. 1–9.

Browning, D., 1991, A *Fundamental Practical Theology*, Minneapolis: Fortress.

Burd, V.A., 1969, *The Winnington Letters of John Ruskin*, Cambridge, Mass: The Belknap Press of Harvard University Press.

Cameron, H., Bhatti, D., Duce, C., Sweeney, J. and Watkins, C., 2010, T*alking about God in Practice: Theological Action Research and Practical Theology*, London: SCM Press.

Cameron, H., Reader, J., Slater, V. with Rowland, C., 2012, *Theological Reflection for Human Flourishing: Pastoral Practice and Public Theology*, London: SCM Press.

Coleridge, S. T., 1956, *Confessions of an Inquiring Spirit*, edited by H. St J. Hart, London: Black.

Cook, E. and Wedderburn, A., eds, 1903–12, T*he Works of John Ruskin*, London: George Allen (referred to as works volume and page number).

Corns, T., Hughes, A. and Loewenstein, D., 2009, T*he Complete Works of Gerrard Winstanley*, Oxford: Oxford University Press.

Cupitt, D., 2016, *Ethics in the Last Days of Humanity*, Salem Oregon: Polebridge Press.

Davidson, D., 2006, *The Essential Davidson*, Oxford: Oxford University Press.

Davies, A., 2006, 'Journeys through the doors of perception: John Ruskin and Willian Blake', *Ruskin Review and Bulletin* 2:2, pp. 24–45.

Dawkins, R., 2006, *The God Delusion*, London: Bantam Press.

Drury, J., 2000, 'Ruskin's way: tout a fait comme un oiseau', in Collini, S., Whitmore, R. and Young, B., eds, *History, Religion, and Culture: British Intellectual History, 1750–1950*, Cambridge: Cambridge University Press, pp. 156–76.

Eagles, S., 2011, *After Ruskin: The Social and Political Legacies of a Victorian Prophet, 1870–1920*, Oxford: Oxford: Oxford University Press.

Eagleton, T., 2007, *Ideology: An Introduction*, London: Verso.

Egerton 3046, Evangelistarium, British Library, Greek Gospel Lectionary with annotations by John Ruskin.

Eliot, G., 2012, *Silas Marner*, London: Penguin.

Eliot, T. S., 1951, 'Tradition and the Individual Talent', *Selected Essays*, 3rd edn, London: Faber and Faber, pp. 13–22.

Farley, E., 1982, *Ecclesiastical Reflection: An Anatomy of Theological Method*, Philadelphia: Fortress Press.

Ferber, M., 1985, *The Social Vision of William Blake*, Princeton: Princeton University Press.

Fontaine, C., 1997, 'The Abusive Bible: On the Use of Feminist Method in Pastoral Contexts', in Brenner-Idan, A. and Fontaine, C., *Feminist Companion to Reading the Bible: Approaches, Methods and Strategies*, Sheffield: Sheffield Academic Press, pp. 84–113.

Frei, H., 1974, *The Eclipse of Biblical Narrative*, New Haven: Yale.

Gadamer, H.-G., 1979, *Truth and Method*, 2nd edn, London: Sheed and Ward.

Gilbert, S. and Gubar, S., 2000, T*he Madwoman in the Attic: The Woman Writer and the Nineteenth-Century Literary Imagination*, 2nd edn, New Haven and London: Yale University Press.

Gorringe, T., 1999, *Karl Barth Against Hegemony: Christian Theology in Context*, Oxford: Oxford University Press.

Graham, E., Walton, H. and Ward, F., 2005, T*heological Reflection: Methods*, London: SCM Press.

Graham, E., 2013, *Between a Rock and a Hard Place: Public Theology in a Post-Secular Age*, London: SCM Press.

Gutiérrez, G., 1983, T*he Power of the Poor in History*, London: SCM Press.

Habermas, J., 1987, *Knowledge and Human Interests*, Oxford: Polity.

Hampson, D., 1990, *Theology and Feminism*, Oxford: Blackwell.

Hampson, D. and Radford Ruether, R., 1987, 'Is There a Place for Feminists in the Christian Church?', *New Blackfriars* 68, pp. 7–24.

Hayter, M., 1987, *The New Eve in Christ: The Use and Abuse of the Bible in the Debate About Women in the Church*, London: SPCK .

Hegel, G.W. F, 1984, *Lectures on the Philosophy of Religion, Vol. 1 Introduction and The Concept of Religion*, ed. Peter C. Hodgson, trans. R. F. Brown *et al.*, Berkeley: University of California Press.

Heidegger, M., 2000, 'Letter on Humanism', *Global Religious Vision*, (2000), 1, pp. 83–109. http://globalvisionpub.com/globaljourneymanager/pdf/139365768.pdf

Hilton, T., 2002, *John Ruskin*, New Haven; London: Yale University Press.

hooks, bell, 1994, *Teaching to Transgress: Education as the Practice of Freedom*, London: Routledge.

Hughes, G., 2008, *God of Surprises*, rev. edn, London: Darton, Longman and Todd.

Ind, J., 1993, *Fat is a Spiritual Issue*, London: Mowbrays.

Jameson, F., 2002, *The Political Unconscious: Narrative as a Socially Symbolic Act*, London: Routledge.

Jaspert, B., 1982, *Karl Barth-Rudolph Bultmann Letters, 1922–1966*, trans. and ed. G. W. Bromiley, Edinburgh: T. & T. Clark.

Käsemann, E., 1973, 'The Problem of New Testament Theology', *New Testament Studies* 19, pp. 235–45.

Käsemann, E., 2010, *On Being a Disciple of the Crucified Nazarene*, Grand Rapids: Erdmans.

King, N., 2004, T*he New Testament Freshly Translated*, Stowmarket: Mayhew.

Larrain, J., 1992, *The Concept of Ideology*, Aldershot: Gregg.

Lash, N., 1986, 'Ideology, Metaphor and Analogy', *Theology on the Way to Emmaus*, London: SCM Press.

Leach, J., 2007, 'Pastoral Theology as Attention', in *Contact: Practical Theology and Pastoral Care* 153, pp. 19–32.

Le Guin, U., 1996, *The Dispossessed: An Ambiguous Utopia*, London: HarperCollins.

Lewis, C. S., 1970, 'Priestesses in the Church?', in *God in the Dock: Essays on Theology and Ethics* , ed. Hooper, W., Grand Rapids, MI: William Eerdmans.

Lewis, J., 2005, Looking for Life: The Role of 'Theo-Ethical Reasoning' in *Paul's Religion*, London: T & T Clark International.

Lomas, P., 1981, T*he Case for a Personal Psychotherapy,* New

York: Oxford University Press.

Lomas, P., 1987, *The Limits of Interpretation*, Harmondsworth: Penguin.

Luft, J. and Ingham, H., 1955, 'The Johari window, a graphic model of interpersonal awareness', Proceedings of the Western Training Laboratory in Group Development, Los Angeles, University of California, Los Angeles.

Marx, K. and Engels, F., 1998, *The German Ideology: Including Theses on Feuerbach and Introduction to the Critique of Political Economy*, Amherst: Prometheus Books.

McGrath, A. and Collicutt McGrath, J., 2007, *The Dawkins Delusion?: Atheist Fundamentalism and the Denial of the Divine*, London: SPCK.

Mesters, C., 1989, *Defenseless Flower*, Maryknoll: Orbis.

Mesters, C., 1993, 'The Use of the Bible in Christian Communities of the Common People', in *The Bible and Liberation*, eds Gottwald, N. and Horsley, R., 2nd edn, Maryknoll: Orbis, pp. 3–16.

Moltmann, J., 2002, *Theology of Hope: On the Ground and the Implications for a Christian Eschatology*, London: SCM Press.

Mosala, I., 1989, *Biblical Hermeneutics and Black Theology in South Africa*, Grand Rapids: Eerdmans.

Munitiz, J. and Endean, P., 2004, *St Ignatius of Loyala: Personal Writings*, London: Penguin.

Myers, C., 2008, *Binding the Strong Man: A Political Reading of Mark's Story of Jesus*, 20th anniversary edn, Maryknoll: Orbis.

Otto, R., 1950, *The Idea of the Holy: An Inquiry into the Non-Rational Factor in the Idea of the Divine and its Relation to the Rational*, Oxford University Press: London.

Patte, D., 2002, 'Can One Be Critical Without Being Autobiographical? The Case of Romans 1:26–27', in Kitszberger, I. R., ed., *Autobiographical Biblical Criticism: Academic Border Crossings – A Hermeneutical Challenge*, Leiden: Deo Publishing, pp. 34–59.

Pattison, S., 2000, 'Some Straw for the Bricks: A Basic Introduction to Theological Reflection', in Woodward, J. and Pattison, S., eds, *The Blackwell Reader in Pastoral and Practical Theology*, Oxford: Blackwell.

Paulson, R., 1982, *Book and Painting: Shakespeare, Milton, and the Bible: Literary Texts and the Emergence of English Painting*, Knoxville: University of Tennessee Press.

Prickett, S., 2009, *Modernity and the Reinvention of Tradition: Backing into the Future*, Cambridge: Cambridge University Press.

Radford Ruether, R., 1983, *Sexism and God-Talk*, Boston: Beacon Press.

Radford Ruether, R., 1985, 'Feminist Interpretation: A Method of Correlation', *Feminist Interpretation of Scripture*, ed. Russell, L. M., Philadelphia: Westminster Press, pp.

111–24.

Radford Ruether, R., 1995, 'Ecofeminism and Healing Ourselves, Healing the Earth', *Feminist Theology* 9, pp. 51–62.

Rowland, C., 1982, *The Open Heaven: A Study of Apocalyptic in Judaism and Early Christianity*, London: SPCK.

Rowland, C. and Corner, M., 1990, *Liberating Exegesis: The Challenge of Liberation Theology to Biblical Studies*, London: SPCK.

Rowland, C., 1994, 'The Revaluation of All Values: Reflections on the Spiritual Exercises' in *Ignatian Spirituality and Mission, The Way Supplement*, pp. 84–91.

Rowland, C. 1996, 'The Interested Interpreter', in Carroll, M., Clines, D. and Davies, P., *The Bible in Human Society*, Sheffield: Sheffield Academic Press, pp. 429–44.

Rowland, C., 2002, *Christian Origins: An Account of the Setting and Character of the Most Important Messianic Sect of Judaism*, rev. edn, London: SPCK.

Rowland, C. and Bennett, Z., 2006, '"Action is the Life of All": New Testament Theology and Practical Theology', in Rowland, C. and Tuckett, C., *The Nature of New Testament Theology: Essays in honour of Robert Morgan*, Oxford: Blackwell, pp. 186–206.

Rowland, C., 2007, T*he Cambridge Companion to Liberation Theology*, 2nd edn, Cambridge: Cambridge University Press.

Rowland, C., 2010, *Blake and the Bible,* London: Yale University Press.

Rowland, C., 2013, 'Liberationist Reading: Popular Interpretation of the Bible in Brazil', in Dell, K. and Joyce, P., *Biblical Interpretation and Method: Essays in Honour of John Barton*, Oxford: Oxford University Press, pp. 133–48.

Rowland, C., 2016a, 'The Book of Revelation: The Apocalypse of Jesus Christ', in Barton, J., ed., T*he Oxford Research Encyclopedia*, New York: Oxford University Press.

Rowland, C., 2016b, 'The Future of Biblical Studies in Higher Education', in Barton, J. and Groves, P., *The New Testament and the Church: Essays in Honour of John Muddiman*, London: Bloomsbury, pp. 78–92.

Ruskin Foundation (Ruskin Library, Lancaster): unpublished material from Ruskin's Diaries.

Scholem, G., 1955, *Major Trends in Jewish Mysticism*, New York: Schocken.

Schüssler Fiorenza, E., 1993, *But She Said: Feminist Practices of Biblical Interpretation*, Boston Massachusetts: Beacon Press.

Schweitzer, A., 1931, *The Quest of the Historical Jesus: A Critical Study of its Progress from Reimarus to Wrede*, London: Black.

Segal, A., 1990, *Paul the Conver*t, New Haven: Yale University Press.

Segundo, J. L., 1976, *The Liberation of Theology*, Maryknoll: Orbis Books

Soskice, J. M., 1993, 'The Truth Looks Different From Here or on Seeking the Unity of Truth From a Diversity of Perspectives', in Regan, H. and Torrance, A., eds., *Christ and Context: The Confrontation Between Gospel and Culture*, Edinburgh: T. & T. Clark, pp. 43–59.

Stringfellow, W., 1973, *An Ethic for Christians and Other Aliens in a Strange Land*, Waco: Word Books.

Stringfellow, W., 1977, *Conscience and Obedience: The Politics of Romans 13 and Revelation 13 in light of the Second Coming*, Waco: Word Books.

Swinton, J. and Mowat, H., 2006, *Practical Theology and Qualitative Research*, London: SCM Press.

Thiselton, A., 1992, N*ew Horizons in Hermeneutics: The Theory and Practice of Transforming Bible Reading*, Grand Rapids, Michigan: Zondervan.

van Braght, T. J., 1950, *Martyrs Mirror*, Scottdale: Herald Press.

Vermes, G., 1993, *The Religion of Jesus the Jew*, London: SCM Press.

Vygotsky, L., 1978, *Mind and Society*, Cambridge, Mass.: Harvard University Press.

Walton, H., 2014, *Writing Methods in Theological Reflection*, London, England: SCM Press.

Walzer, M., 1985, *Exodus and Revolution*, New York: Basic.

Wilmer, C., 1985, *John Ruskin: Unto this Last and Other Writings*, London: Penguin.

Wolff, J., 2016, 'Why my philosophy students will be working together for a change', *Guardian*, 18 January 2016.

Woodhead, L., 2004, *Christianity: A Very Short Introduction*, Oxford: Oxford University Press.

Žižek, S., 2003, T*he Puppet and the Dwarf: The Perverse Core of Christianity*, London: MIT Press.

Biblical Index

Revelation (continued)

Subject Index